7.24 —

Taste the Freedom!

MW00325822

A

CHEF

IS

BORN

I love this book! Otto's recipe for life is as warm and nutritious as his recipes for food! He delights us with musical pairings, hilarious anecdotes, poems, proverbs, even a White House recipe. Delicious!

MARCIA GAY HARDEN
ACADEMY AWARD WINNING ACTRESS

A fun read about becoming a chef, an instructor, and believer. Motivated by others on his journey including old school restauranteurs and the swagger and bravado of Bruce Springsteen. The interwoven personal recipes are a nice touch.

DAVID BURKE
JAMES BEARD AWARD WINNER,
RESTAURATEUR, PATENT HOLDER, AND CULINARY PRANKSTER

A fascinating heartfelt story. Individual, yet universal in its expression. Otto's love of food combined with his passion for cooking as an offering to others, gives new meaning to Brillat-Saverin's, the famous eighteenth century gastronome's statement, "There is no place like the table to reconcile mind and body to a life that is necessarily too short and too indifferent." This book is an inspiration for all.

BARRY WINE
CHEF, FORMER OWNER OF *THE QUILTED GIRAFFE*

Hail to the Chef! Otto Borsich serves up an inspiring, delicious, and nourishing feast in *A Chef is Born*. You will ask for seconds.

DR. CONNIE MARIANO
WHITE HOUSE PHYSICIAN, REAR ADMIRAL, USN (RETIRED)
AUTHOR OF "THE WHITE HOUSE DOCTOR: MY PATIENTS WERE PRESIDENTS"

Otto is a master wordsmith who keeps the reader enthralled through each phase of his food journey. Then he cleverly ends each chapter with recipes that fit into the story line. The only problem I have with the book is when I'm reading at night in bed. I want to go into the kitchen and start making the recipes!

DEAN FEARING
CHEF-OWNER, *FEARING'S RESTAURANT*
AND JAMES BEARD AWARD WINNER

Otto is an eccentric soul, a great storyteller combining history, music, recipes, and scripture. This is a superlative memoir. Like a three star Michelin meal, you will never forget Otto. Now the world will get to know the great friend that I've had the pleasure of knowing for decades. Within these pages is his story, in his words. No one better to tell it.

JOSEPH KELLER
CHEF-OWNER, *COMPANY OF THE CAULDRON*
NANTUCKET, MASSACHUSETTS

the publishing CIRCLE

For permission requests, write to the publisher, addressed
"Attention: Permissions Coordinator," at the address below.

admin@ThePublishingCircle.com
or
THE PUBLISHING CIRCLE, LLC
Regarding: Otto Borsich
19215 SE 34th Street
Suite 106-347
Camas, Washington 98607

This book is a work of creative nonfiction. The events are portrayed to the
best of Otto Borsich's memory. Some names and identifying details have
been changed to protect the privacy of the people involved. The story, the
experiences, the words, and opinions are the author's alone.

The publisher is not responsible for the author's website, other mentioned
websites, dead or expired links to any website, redirected links, or content
of any website that is not owned by the publisher.

Scriptures taken from the *The Holy Bible: King James Version*.

A CHEF IS BORN / Otto Borsich
ISBN 978-1-947398-28-3 (paperback)
ISBN 978-1-947398-55-9 (hardcover)
FIRST EDITION

CREDITS:
Cover and page 298 photo by Noelle Guerry, Noelle Guerry Photography
Back cover photo courtesy of the Borsich family archives
Illustration of Anthony Bourdain (page 254) ©Rolando Diaz
    (Google: Rolando Diaz/Artist)
Book design by Michele Uplinger

The author will donate a portion of the proceeds from this book
to @WhyHunger.

*This book is in memory
of my mother, Rose, aka Rosie.
A great cook who unfailingly
delivered dinner every night.*
Rest in Peace, Mom

JULY 12, 1927 – OCTOBER 15, 2004

■

"This is not a profession that you choose.
It chooses you."

NORMAN VAN AKEN

■

TABLE OF CONTENTS

INTRODUCTION

T HAS BEEN SAID THAT EVERYONE has at least one book in them. This book has been a work in progress for years. The seed was planted when I was a Chef Instructor at the Culinary Institute of America (CIA), Hyde Park Campus. While employed there, I enrolled in some classes. One class was Cuisine and Cultures, a wonderful class that delved into the fascinating and sometimes forbidden world of food, exploring the rich history and traditions of why people eat what they do. After a 55-year gestation period, it is time to record the story of Otto, a boy born to be a chef.

The main reason I took the class was because of the Professor, Dr. Krishnendu Ray. Affectionately known as K. Ray, a short, bespectacled, friendly man of Eastern Indian ancestry, he was known as the best teacher on campus. Holding a BA and MA in political science, as well as an MA and Ph.D. in sociology, K. Ray remains the most intelligent individual I have met along this journey called life.

About halfway through the 15-week course, K. Ray said to me, "I want to see you after class."

Uh-oh, I thought. This was no longer K. Ray the friend, the CIA colleague, the teachers' union representative. It was Professor Ray, seeking Student Borsich after class. I sat fidgeting in the classroom, along with the cadre of twenty-somethings pursuing their bachelor's in culinary or baking and pastry arts. What had I done? Why did he want to see me? As I nervously watched the clock tick, 4:00 p.m. finally hit—class dismissed. I deliberately waited for all the youngsters to exit before walking up to K. Ray's desk. "Yes, K. Ray? You wanted to see me?" I said, sheepishly.

"I've been reading your reports with great interest," he said. "You have a distinct writing style: engaging, highly opinionated. I encourage you to keep writing because you will get noticed. All you need is one best seller and you're set for life."

Wow! What a great compliment from a man who had garnered my complete respect and admiration. I took his advice and ran with it. Thus began my contributions to *La Papillote,* the CIA student newspaper, where I brought a faculty perspective about life at *The World's Greatest Cooking School.* I eventually left the CIA and in doing so stopped writing for the most part, but always knew I would put pen to paper again someday.

On August 23, 2009, that day arrived. I was in my hometown of Vermilion, Ohio, visiting Dad who would turn eighty-two in a matter of days. We were having dinner at Quaker State and Lube. It sounds like a gas station, but it's actually a filling station of a different sort. Three decades earlier, McGarvey's Restaurant proudly stood there. McGarvey's was my first restaurant job, the place where I began to cut my teeth on the wonderful world of food. As Dad and I savored our yellow perch dinner while overlooking the scenic Vermilion River, I told him about K. Ray's words from years past. With his piercing blue eyes, he looked at me and simply said, "I hope I get to read that book before I go."

The greatest mother of all memory loss is Father Time. The grains of sand trickling through my life's hourglass at times created a dune I had to traverse. Everything in this book is true, it is not exact word-for-word, and it would be impossible to make it so. The names have been changed to protect the innocent and the stupid. My greatest joy is for you to have as much fun reading it as I did writing it. To stay inspired and be an inspiration.

Dad, thanks for the inspiration you have always been: it is an honor, a privilege, and a responsibility to be your namesake. I have faith that I'll be as great a man as you are or die trying. Even if I reach fifty percent of your awesomeness, I'll be happy. This book is also for you.

Love,

Otto two

FOREWORD

OD NEVER SAYS, "OOPS." We are all born with a purpose. You are here for a reason. You are unique. There was never anyone exactly like you before you were born. There will never be anyone exactly like you after you die. Each of us is distinctly diverse. Everyone is exceptional, as intricate, delicate, and spectacular as a snowflake. Alone we are fragile souls, but like snowflakes, we are powerful when we stick together. Despite our sharp differences that slash through religious, social, economic, ethnic, gender, and political playing fields, we are connected. Nowhere is this more evident than with the food we eat. It nourishes and sustains us. The simple act of breaking bread is as ancient as mankind. Food is the great equalizer. The single common thread that weaves the multihued tapestry of humanity. As a chef, I have been blessed to travel, explore faraway places and consume cuisines and cultures that many people merely dream about. In doing so, my spiritual thirst remains unquenched. There is so much to see and do and learn, experiences like these deepen one's level of acceptance and tolerance. Since leaving my small hometown over forty years ago to discover the world, I have continually encountered a single commonality: we are far more alike than we are different. We all yearn for the same things: to live freely in peace; to be allowed to express ourselves creatively; to have the opportunity to receive a quality education; to have access to proper medical care; and to have fresh food and safe drinking water. This book is about a blessed soul and a mission heavenly assigned before breeching the birth canal. I humbly and enthusiastically embrace this calling. After what essentially amounts to a lifetime of pursuing it, my greatest hope is this book will be the spark that starts a fire in you. To create an inferno of change and make your dream come true. As stated earlier, we are all born with a purpose and we have a finite time on Earth to fulfill that purpose. However, purpose is not enough: *mission accomplished* is! I heartily wish you good luck and Godspeed on accomplishing your mission.

∎

Nothing is impossible.

With God all things are possible.
MARK 10:27

∎

Taste the Freedom!

A CHEF IS BORN

AN OTTO-BIOGRAPHY

OTTO G. BORSICH II

CHAPTER 1

BELIEVE

MUSICAL PAIRING: Goes great with "I Believe"
MALI MUSIC, VINTAGE 2014

WAS RAISED IN THE TINY TOWNSHIP of Brownhelm, a town the size of a postage stamp, thirty miles west of Cleveland and a skipping stone away from Lake Erie.

During the Great Depression, the leaders of this agricultural hamlet decided to get together and provide for everyone in the village who was struggling due to the major economic downturn that affected the entire world like an economic El Niño. Hopelessness had swept through America with the force of a tsunami, drowning people in a sea of despair. Unemployment soared, and bread lines were the norm from one-horse towns to every bustling metropolis.

In 1931, a little girl moved the heart of Reverend Albrecht of the Brownhelm Congregational Church, telling him that some families would have no Christmas at all. He organized the town folk, gathering them together to repair donated second-hand toys. They also produced fresh baked goods and included winter fruits and preserves in gift baskets. On Christmas Eve, the men of Brownhelm donned the traditional St. Nick attire and set out by car, truck, tractor, and horse and buggy to deliver the gifts to the thirty homes in the township. In the still twilight of the Midwestern chill, Santa Claus arrived, not with reindeer, but on a John Deere. He gleefully went door to door spreading cheer, hope, treats, sustenance, and—in the true sense of Christmas—showed the heart of what it meant to give lovingly and unconditionally.

The actions of these compassionate souls inaugurated a neighborhood tradition that continues to this day and is now in its eighty-eighth year. On its golden anniversary in 1981, the heartwarming story was featured on *CBS Evening News* with Dan Rather. The town's resiliency, the inner strength to overcome adversity and prevail against all odds, the ability to adapt and overcome, the desire to conquer all obstacles and triumphantly hurdle those challenges with the grace and power of Jackie Joyner-Kersee, is something that exists not only in the citizens of Brownhelm, but in each and every one of us. It is intestinal fortitude, moxie, mental toughness, and the pioneering spirit that built America. That indescribable specialness, that inexplicable intangible, is what makes America great, and the envy of every other nation in the global village.

This year Santa will visit nine-hundred homes in Brownhelm. There are eighteen routes, eighteen Santas, eighteen drivers, eighteen route chairmen, and scores of everyday heroes ensuring a Merry Christmas to all. Santa continues to send a Christmas card every year to all the local men and women in uniform, too.

Christmas is not about opening presents. It's about opening minds. It's not about wrapping gifts, it's about being the gift. As a bumpkin growing up in Brownhelm, I believed in Santa Claus. After all, he delivered the goods to my house every Christmas Eve. Since leaving my idyllic hometown forty years ago, I still believe in Santa. I know on December 24 in Brownhelm, at 2025 Sunnyside Road, in the white colonial dream house my father built, Santa Claus will arrive to spread holiday cheer. Santa Claus is real—indubitably real. All you have to do is believe.

■

First, think.
Second, believe.
Third, dream.
And finally, dare.
WALT DISNEY

Be not afraid, only believe.
MARK 5:36

■

THIS TASTY TREAT TRANSPORTS me to Brownhelm and the true meaning of Christmas.

I'm uncertain how this German classic cookie was introduced into my mom's heavy Italian repertoire. It was a holiday favorite and one Santa always received when visiting the Borsich family. When I was a kid, I referred to it as a snowball cookie. It's a lot easier to say than *Pfeffernüsse*. I love the snap of the warm spices, the heat of the peppercorn, and the powdery sugar that lingers on your lips. For a little cookie, it packs a punch. *Pferrernüsse* translates to pepper nuts.

PFEFFERNÜSSE

2¼ cups all-purpose flour

½ teaspoon salt

½ teaspoon crushed anise seed

¼ teaspoon fresh ground pepper

¾ teaspoon ground cinnamon

½ teaspoon ground allspice

¼ teaspoon fresh ground nutmeg

¼ teaspoon ground cloves

¼ teaspoon baking soda

½ cup, (one stick) of sweet butter, room temperature

¾ cup firmly packed light brown sugar

1 large egg

¼ cup molasses

1¼ cups powdered sugar

Preheat oven to 350°F. Line two baking sheets with parchment paper. Place the powdered sugar in a brown paper bag.

In a medium bowl, combine the first nine ingredients and set aside.

Place butter, brown sugar and molasses in the bowl of an electric mixer. Beat on medium speed until fluffy. Add egg and vanilla and continue to beat until fully incorporated. With the mixer on low, add the flour mixture until just combined. Scoop out dough in tablespoons, roll into balls, and arrange 1½ inches apart on a prepared baking sheet.

Bake about 15 minutes until the cookies are golden and firm to the touch with slight cracking. Rotate the sheets halfway through the cooking time. Transfer the sheets to a wire rack and cool slightly. While still warm and working in small batches, place some cookies in the paper bag with the powdered sugar and shake gently until well coated. Remove cookies from bag and let them cool completely on a wire rack. Once cool, store in an airtight container.

Serves 12–15 people.

Taste the Freedom.

CHAPTER 2

THE MIRACULOUS BEGINNING

MUSICAL PAIRING: Goes great with "God Bless the Child"
BILLIE HOLIDAY, VINTAGE 1941

DON'T EXPECT MIRACLES; I rely on them. That reliance was formed at birth, wondrously woven within the umbilical cord and transcribed into my DNA. I exited the birth canal somewhere near the stroke of eleven the morning of April 30, 1960. I was born a Taurus and that's no bull. Just minutes old, I would need the brute strength of a thousand bulls to stampede the poison overrunning my newborn body.

My mother, Rosie, had already birthed four children, or six if you count the twins miscarried the year before. Back then, giving an enema to a woman before she went into the delivery room was a routine procedure. The muscles an expectant mother uses to push the baby out are the same ones used to defecate. When that mother is pushing with the ferocity of an NFL lineman, other bodily functions may be triggered. To prevent a bowel movement, an enema is administered as a precautionary measure.

As my mother lay in her bed at St. Joseph's Hospital in Lorain, Ohio, she knew it was time for her fifth child to make his way out of the womb, to squeeze his way through the birthing tunnel, and safely exit into the hands of Dr. Michael Varga-Sinka, the awaiting physician. Rosie hit the button to notify the nurse's desk that she needed help. Enter Nurse Barian, Barb Barian. As thick as a sequoia stump and the personification of a Soviet Bloc Olympic weight lifter. Her bedside manner possessed all the pleasantries of a full bedpan. The nurse entered my mother's room and asked, "What's wrong?" My mother said, "I am ready to have the baby right now." I'm sure there was some discussion about labor pains, contractions, and intervals. If I were a betting embryo I would not bet against Rosie. After all, I'm her fifth child. If anybody knew her body and could tell when the baby was going to breach the birth canal, it was my mother, not some starched-hat, white-hose-wearing newbie out of nursing school. "I'll be right back," said Nurse Barian, and back she was, with a liquid-filled plastic bottle fitted with an extended tip. Rosie point-blank refused to take the enema. Unfortunately, Barian's limited nursing skills won out over my mother's years of real-life experience.

She administered an enema to my mother just moments before my birth. Call it woman's intuition, the psychic powers Rosie claimed to have, the experience of previously birthing four children, or quite simply the powerful bond between mother and child, but one thing Rosie knew—something was wrong. Horrifically wrong. During the nurse's insistence on the enema and Rosie's resistance, a struggle occurred, and the enema was inserted vaginally.

The enema breached the protective womb and invaded my infantile organism. My body absorbed a harsh cocktail of chemicals designed to flush out one's bowels. Enemas work on a saline principal to draw excess moisture from the body to soften stools. One of the ingredients, ethylenediaminetetraacetic acid, (EDTA), is the same chemical used to dissolve lime scale. The solution was literally dehydrating my unborn body of vital fluids while viciously attacking my fragile immune system. No amount of huffing and puffing, pushing and forcing by Momma would eradicate the toxicity from my tender tissues. Like a catcher with his mitt in the dirt, Dr. Varga-Sinka positioned his hands to grab and welcome me to the world. A snip of the umbilical cord and I was rushed to ICU, Code Blue.

My mother had not even seen her fifth child yet, but she knew something horrible had happened. They wrapped and whisked me away faster than you could say rock-a-bye baby. You know the old joke; when you were born, you were so ugly they slapped your mama. My childbirth represented that punch line. I recall my mother telling me I was so unsightly, forty-eight hours passed before she laid eyes on me. The medical team had given up on me from the get-go and advised my parents to make funeral arrangements. "Your son is not going to make it, I'm sorry," they said, while simultaneously preparing my birth and death certificate. I had a premature date with the Grim Reaper, yet the Grim Reaper met his match with Momma, and God. A devout Roman Catholic, my mother's faith was so robust she named me Otto with good reason. She believed no son of hers named after his father would perish from this earth. That's why I was given the name Otto George Borsich.

The hospital all but administered last rites, and were prepared to place me in the kiddie coffin and called it a day. Yet there were two people and a force they didn't count on—Momma, God, and prayer. A wait-and-see attitude prevailed, but the forecast was bleak. I was clinging to life by a shred of a thread.

My parents, Dr. Varga-Sinka, and a nurse entered the pediatric ICU. Inside the somber and spotlessly clean environment, a few sickly newborns lay in incubators. My mother knew immediately which one I was and understood why the hospital refused to show me to her. I was grossly discolored in varying shades of purple and green, shriveled like a prune, dormant and dehydrated. There I lay, listless, in a sterile, climate-controlled unit. I went from my mother's oven to an incubator. From natural, protective moist housing to an arid, man-made plastic shell plugged into an electrical outlet to replicate the warmth of my mother's womb. Even though that apparatus seems antiquated by today's standards, I'm sure vital signs were monitored, complete with bells and whistles sounding the alarm if things grew more dangerously wrong than they already were.

My mother and father wanted to hold me. All they were allowed to do was put their hands on the plastic housing and feel the warmth from the electronic lifeline. There were more questions than answers as the doctor explained to my parents that I had been poisoned and my lungs were filled with the fluid from the enema. The doctor did not mince words. He prepared my parents for the worst. There was little my parents could do; now my fate rested with the medical team of St. Joseph's Hospital, God, and prayer. I am certain my mother was on her knees day and night, palms clenched tightly around a rosary, praying for a miracle.

As my dear friend and spiritual mentor, Arthur Caliandro, would say, "When you pray, God has three answers: yes, no, and wait a while." Wait Momma did. In between daily visits to the hospital, Momma kept her mind off me by staying busy getting my older siblings ready for school, filling my dad's lunchbox, cooking dinner, doing dishes and laundry and cleaning house. Days turned into weeks and then into a month. Over that long separation, the warmth of the incubator, the steady nourishment of the IV, and the care from St. Joseph's medical team made it possible for me to sit here today and tell the story of my miraculous beginning. But the medical care can't hold a candle to the power of a mother's prayer and God's mercy. God answered my mother's prayers and bestowed a purposeful life that is mine alone. He is not done with me—far from it. My *miraculous beginning* was just that.

■

The child must know that he is a miracle, that since the beginning of the world there hasn't been, and until the end of the world there will not be, another child like him.

PABLO CASALS

Before I formed thee in the belly I knew thee; and before thou camest forth out of the womb I sanctified thee, and I ordained thee a prophet unto the nations.

JEREMIAH 1:5

■

ONCE I WAS WELL BEYOND the dangers of the toxic birth, Dr. Varga-Sinka told my mother, "Feed him peanut butter, butter, and ice cream to fatten him up." So I chose this recipe, CHOCOLATE PEANUT BUTTER SOUFFLÉ, to commemorate my birth. In French, *soufflé* translates to "breathe." God's sweet kiss of life resuscitated my body and soul into a miraculous beginning.

CHOCOLATE PEANUT BUTTER SOUFFLÉ

PEANUT BUTTER BASE:

1½ cups whole milk

½ cup heavy cream

1 large egg

1 large egg yolk

⅓ cup sugar

1 tablespoon cornstarch

1 tablespoon all-purpose flour

½ cup smooth peanut butter (do not use fresh ground)

pinch of salt, to taste

CHOCOLATE SOUFFLÉ:

10 ounces bittersweet or semisweet chocolate, chopped
(use a high-quality chocolate like Valrhona or Callebaut)

5 tablespoons sweet butter

5 large egg yolks

7 tablespoons water

¼ cup whole milk
2 tablespoons unsweetened cocoa powder
4 large egg whites, room temperature
½ teaspoon cream of tartar
pinch of salt
½ cup sugar

PEANUT BUTTER BASE: Bring milk and heavy cream to a simmer in a saucepan; do not boil. Whisk egg and yolk together. Add sugar, cornstarch, and flour to eggs; whisk to blend. Gradually whisk hot milk-cream mixture into egg mixture to temper it, then return to saucepan. Bring mixture to a boil over medium-high heat, whisking constantly. Boil 1 minute, still whisking. Remove from heat. Whisk peanut butter into hot base. Season with salt. Place plastic wrap directly onto the surface of base. Chill until cold, at least 3 hours or overnight. The base can be made 24 hours in advance.

CHOCOLATE SOUFFLÉ: Preheat oven to 350°F. Butter and sprinkle sugar into eight 3/4-cup ramekins or custard cups, or one large deep round casserole, similar to a large ramekin. Place chocolate and butter in large metal bowl. Set bowl over saucepan of simmering water; stir until mixture is smooth. Remove from heat and cool to room temperature. Whisk yolks, water, milk, and cocoa in medium bowl until cocoa dissolves. Using electric mixer, beat egg whites, cream of tartar, and salt until frothy. With mixer running, gradually add sugar to egg-white mixture. Whip until shiny peaks form, about 3 minutes. With a rubber spatula fold yolk mixture into the whites. Fold the egg mixture into the chocolate.

Fill cups or baking dish halfway with soufflé mixture. Spoon rounded tablespoons of the peanut butter base into the center of each. Spoon remaining soufflé mixture on top to cover and fill ramekins. Bake until soufflés rise about 1 inch above dish and are set in center, about 22–24 minutes. Serve immediately.

Serves 8.

Taste the Freedom.

CHAPTER 3

THE SINGER, THE STRUDEL, & GRANDMA B

MUSICAL PAIRING: Goes great with "Vogue"
MADONNA, VINTAGE 1990

RANDMA BORSICH WAS CUT FROM a different cloth. The shirts she made for her husband and three sons were made entirely by hand on a manual foot-powered old-school Singer sewing machine. She never used a pattern. Like a gifted musician playing by ear, Grandma B could orchestrate a shirt by eye, creating a garment that would rival the finest from Savile Row tailors.

I remember that sewing machine with fondness. In large part, it was instrumental in developing my sense of style.

Even as a tot, I marveled at its beauty. Grandma kept the sewing machine at the rear of the dining room in front of the window that looked onto the backyard. When not in use, which wasn't often, the machine doubled as a desk. Housed in an oak cabinet with cast-iron accents, the machine had iron legs and a metal bracket that crisscrossed the framework to provide support.

The sewing machine itself was beautiful, a mechanical masterpiece with ebony luster and elaborate gold scrollwork. It reminded me of a Cadillac from yesteryear. Big, bold, beautiful, an elegant and enduring design that just screamed, *Take me for a ride!* . . . and ride it Grandma did.

Sometimes Grandma would take me for a ride on the Singer. My safety belt was her left arm wrapped around my waist as I straddled her thigh. She would guide the pedal, giving it gas to activate the needle at low speed to maneuver curves such as those on a collar or cuffs. At other times, she revved up when finishing a long strip on the front of the shirt where the buttons would be. I liked that part the best. Without breaking a sweat, and smiling all the way down the straightaway, Grandma would pump that peddle faster than a toe-tapping, banjo-pickin' hillbilly.

"Faster, Grandma! Faster!" I'd shriek.

"Vvvvvrrrrrroooooommmmm," she'd buzz into my ear, mimicking the roaring engine of a Cadillac. I felt her love hum all the way to my racing heart.

I marveled at how Grandma took these enormous shears,

seemingly as long as my arm, and methodically cut the fabric. Miraculously, she would craft a shirt faster than you could say Brooks Brothers. At an early age, I learned the difference between custom-made and off-the-rack, and off-the-rack would never cut it for this customized kid.

In addition to having an early influence on my sense of style, Grandma B provided my first food memory: apple strudel, a staple in the Borsich household. Grandma was as adept at making strudel as she was at fabricating cloth into clothes. Anyone who has made strudel from scratch knows it is a laborious, time-consuming task. You can take a shortcut and use phyllo dough, but there is no substitute for scratch. The ingredients are simple enough: flour, salt, water, and oil. Sift the dry ingredients, then add the water and oil. The water binds the flour and salt together, and the oil adds elasticity, essential when stretching the dough.

I recall how Grandma manhandled the dough. To get a commanding view, I stood tall, my feet on the seat of a dining room chair. Grandma would pick up the dough ball and, with the force of Hulk Hogan, slam it onto the matted dining room table. In between slams, she'd knead the dough, working it with the base of her palms, pushing forward and away from her toward the center of the table. After she had fully extended her outstretched arms, she'd rotate the dough and bring it back to the edge of the table. She repeated this process four or five times. She would then pick up the dough ball, hold it high, and crash it onto the table with another hand-slam. Again, and again, kneading and slamming,

slamming and kneading. The dough took a beating. I watched in amazement as Grandma owned that dough, continuously flogging it like a pirate thrashing a cabin boy.

The excessive beating was necessary: Grandma was intensifying the gluten and aligning the starch molecules to provide strength to the dough with every twist, turn, and slam. She beat it so severely until miniscule blisters were formed on the dough. When that happened, it was time for the dough to rest. The dough rested for perhaps an hour or two, then it would be easier to roll out and eventually stretch.

While the dough relaxed, Grandma prepared the apple mixture for the filling. She liked to use Granny Smith apples because of their tartness and because they retained their shape during baking. With peeler in hand, I helped skin the apples. With the skill of a professional chef, Grandma diced inch-thick apple pieces with uniform precision. Next, raisins, chopped walnuts, sugar, and cinnamon were tossed with the fruit. I remember the taste of that apple mixture—teeth-clenching tart and crispy. The grit of sugar was like sweet sand romanced with the perfume of cinnamon. I loved the texture, that bite, the tang, the mouth-watering taste of God's little green apple. It was high on the pucker-power meter, but sweet enough for a smile of delight from this boy who was born to be a chef. Learning how to make strudel from scratch from Grandma B was my first cooking lesson.

With the filling made and the dough well rested, it was now time to get rolling. Grandma would retrieve her large weathered rolling pin from a kitchen drawer. It was solid wood, a good four inches in diameter. Grandma gave me the rolling pin to hold onto and I held it by the handle vertically and spun it around with my free hand. Grandma then placed a bedsheet on top of the large dining room table. With a handful of Gold Medal All-Purpose Flour and a short sweeping motion as if skipping stones, she would quickly release the flour and lightly dust the sheet. When Grandma placed the sheet over the table, it nearly hung to floor level. From my viewpoint, the table, which comfortably seated twelve, looked humongous. Grandma would begin rolling the dough, from the center outward. During the rolling process, I would hang out under the massive table, swaddled by the king-size sheet, immersed in my own little world of make-believe.

I entertained myself by playing my own version of Knights of the Round Table. When I grew up, America truly was the land of hope and dreams. Any child could grow up to be whatever they wanted to be, whether it was President of the United States of America, or an astronaut. I believed it then; I believe it now. Beneath the table, I romanticized about Camelot, about King Arthur and the Knights of the Round Table. I was one of King Arthur's knights! A heroic figure in the most fanciful suit of armor, mounted on a white stallion, lance in hand, I would charge my raging thoroughbred on a collision course with a ferocious, fire-breathing dragon. At maximum speed and in adrenaline overload, I'd thrust the spiked shaft through the dragon's protective body armor. Scoring a direct hit, a geyser of crimson would erupt, staining the stallion's snow-white coat. After a quick about-face, I'd dismount my steed, which would then rear up on hind legs and give an exuberant, *neigh!* My Excalibur grasped in a double-handed grip, I'd rotate into a full discus-thrower windup, spinning madly, laser focused on the giraffe-sized neck of the dragon. Leaping in one fell swoop, I'd swing the supernatural sword and sever the head of the dastardly beast. No sooner had I cut the head off the dragon than Grandma would raise the curtain on my fantasyland. Time to stretch out the dough.

As I crawled out from underneath the table, Grandma would pick me up and stand me on one of the dining room chairs. The other chairs had been removed in preparation for stretching the dough. The rolling pin had accomplished as much as it could, so now my grandmother placed her gnarled fingers in the center of the table under the dough, palms upward. Gently, but confidently, Grandma pulled the dough. This took great skill. Grandma had years of practice, no doubt learning the finer points from her own mother, a strudel maestro. Grandma used her hands to delicately pull the dough, stretching the elastic mass to new borders and beyond as the dough hung over the edges of the table. Slowly and steadily, she walked the circumference of the table with the dough hugging the tops of her hands. She coaxed the dough into a delicate, translucent sheet.

"Bring me the newspaper, Otto," she'd say.

I'd jump off the seat and scamper into the living room, pick up the *Lorain Journal,* and bring it to Grandma. She'd move the chair close to the table and stand me on it. With a folded section of paper in her hand, she'd pick up the dough and place the newspaper under it. "Tin tin," she'd announce, her thick, Central European accent distorting "thin thin." The newspaper served as the instrument for the sheerness test. Grandma stretched that dough so thin the black newsprint was visible through the manila-skinned surface. Then, and only then, was Grandma ready to add the apple filling and roll the strudel. Like a painter working a colossal canvas, she brushed the delicate pastry ever so gently with melted butter. Next, she liberally tossed breadcrumbs from top to bottom and side to side. The miniscule bits of dry bread served as a barrier and provided the crispness and layers associated with this Hungarian delicacy.

Strudel is baklava's majestic cousin. The Turks of the Ottoman Empire brought the honey-laden pistachio baklava first to Hungary, then to Austria, during the Habsburg Empire (1278–1789). The innovative Austro-Hungarian Sultans of Sweet put their spin on it by rolling, not layering, the dough, then replacing nuts and syrup with apples, cinnamon and sugar—voila! The national dessert of Austria and Hungary was born. Today, apple strudel reigns honorably as the dessert of choice in that ancient kingdom.

The word strudel translates to "swirl" or "whirlpool," which relates to the rolling process. Grandma would arrange the apples toward one end of the dough in a pile as broad as a telephone pole. Grabbing the end of the bedsheet she would pull upward on the fabric and push it forward to roll the dough around the apples until the dough completely encircled the apples, thus creating the swirling effect. The bulging log of goodness was too big for any cookie tray Grandma owned. She'd carefully form the strudel into a U-shape, so the baking sheet could accommodate the girth and length of the soon-to-be-baked apple pastry.

The rousing aroma of cinnamon-scented apples would permeate the entire house. All the love Grandma B put into the strudel vaporized and gently flowed out of the oven like a spicy trade wind tickling our noses and triggering our senses. Truly heaven scent. The whiff of that lingering essence was a warning shot fired across the bow of my taste buds. In short order, the strudel would meet my mouth, providing pleasure to my pint-sized palate. The warm tenderness of the apples, the lush creaminess of the vanilla bean ice cream and the delicateness of the crisp exterior, melded exquisitely. A divine dessert created by the Gastronomic Gods for mere mortals to indulge, reminding us of the joy and sexiness of simplicity.

Grandma B was quite a lady, wife, mother, and grandmother, and equally as skilled as an old-world artisan. My dad, Otto Sr., said he only heard her utter a profanity once: "Son of a bitch." Dad didn't recall what prompted this outburst, but to hear your parent(s) swear only once in a lifetime, well, we need more parents like that today. Grandma surrendered her Hungarian National status and became a U.S. citizen in 1940. My dad said she told him that was the happiest day of her life.

Grandma B moved from the Singer to the strudel like

a first-class conductor skilled in every instrument in the orchestra. Her skillset was extraordinary, downright magical. Elizabeth Vas Borsich. Vas translates as "iron," and Grandma was indeed as tough as iron. She lived to be ninety-one. When she was getting up in years, she once jokingly asked my dad, "Where did the time go?"

Thanks for the Singer, the strudel, and the power to dream, Grandma B! —SEPTEMBER 23, 1895 – FEBRUARY 11, 1987 RIP

∎

Nobody can do for little children what grandparents do. Grandparents sort of sprinkle stardust over the lives of little children.

ALEX HALEY

And he hath filled him with the spirit of God, in wisdom, in understanding, and in knowledge, and in all manner of workmanship; And to devise curious works, to work in gold, and in silver, and in brass.

EXODUS 35:31-32

∎

GRANDMA B'S APPLE STRUDEL

DOUGH:

2½ cups flour

3 tablespoons vegetable oil

10 to 12 tablespoons water

FILLING:

3 Granny Smith apples peeled, seeded, and diced into large chunks

½ cup raisins

½ cup walnuts

1 tablespoon lemon juice

¾ cup sugar

1 teaspoon cinnamon

pinch of salt

½ cup cake crumbs or bread crumbs

melted butter

Preheat oven to 425°. Make a well in the flour in a large bowl or on a countertop. Add the oil and water and begin to mix by hand until a smooth, elastic dough is formed, about 5 minutes. Set aside to relax the dough for 30 to 60 minutes.

After the dough has rested, roll it out on a cutting board into a rectangle about 10 by 14 inches. You will need a large, clean piece of fabric (a bedsheet works great). Place it over your kitchen table. Transfer the dough onto the center of the table. With your fingertips together and working from the very center, reach under the dough and begin to stretch it outward, toward you and the edge of the table. Keep stretching the dough, working completely around the table with your fingertips or use the upper part of your palms to pull the dough in larger swatches. You eventually want a piece of dough about 20 by 30 inches. If the dough tears, just patch it up with some dough from the edge. To assess its thinness, give the dough the newspaper test (a magazine will also do the trick).

Once you have the dough rolled out, work quickly to peel, core and cut the apples. Add the lemon, sugar, cinnamon, nuts, and raisins. Best to do this step after the dough is rolled, otherwise the sugar and lemon juice leach out the juice of the apple, making it difficult to roll. Butter the dough, sprinkle the crumbs, and spread the apples about 8 inches from the edge of one end and about 3 inches from either side. You want an even, log-shaped mound of apples. Using the end of the fabric, carefully bring (or place) the dough over the top of the apple mixture, separating the dough from the fabric as you go. Keep rolling the strudel forward with the sheet. The dough is far too delicate to roll by hand. At the halfway point of rolling the dough, tuck or fold in the ends, burrito style, and continue to roll until you have reached the other end. Roll the strudel onto a parchment-lined baking sheet. If the strudel is too large for the baking sheet, curve it into a U-shape to make it fit. Brush with melted butter and bake for 20 minutes at 425°, then reduce the heat to 350°F for another 10 to 15 minutes until pastry is golden brown. Serve warm with ice cream or whipped cream.

Serves 8–10.

Taste the Freedom.

CHAPTER 4

MOM & DAD

MUSICAL PAIRING: Goes great with "Kiss an Angel Good Morning"
CHARLIE PRIDE, VINTAGE, 1971

"WHY DO YOU DO THAT?" my youngest brother, Mike, the baby of the family, asked our mother.

"Do what?" she replied.

"Every morning, when Dad goes to work, you go to the window and wave goodbye. Then you run over to the opposite window and wave goodbye again as he makes the turn. Isn't once enough?"

"That might be the last time I ever see your father."

That was their ritual every day, evidence of their devotion—their religion was indulging one another.

∎

YEARS BEFORE THEY MET, my father saw the world while

still in his teens. He served for three years in the United States Merchant Marines. During that time, he completed an eleven-month worldwide cruise onboard the T2 tanker, *Eleazar Lord,* out of Mobile Bay, Alabama. He shipped out on August 14, 1945, the day WWII ended. I loved the stories of his travels to over sixty countries.

Dad had an old blue, chipped porcelain pot with a lid and a black steel arc handle. That pot was used by my grandfather as a lunch pail when he used to work at the shipyard when my father was a boy. His father worked at American Ship and helped build the gigantic vessels that sailed to faraway lands. Perhaps that is where my dad got the notion to join the Merchant Marines.

I never met my Grandfather Borsich. He died in May 1962, when I was just two years old. But I loved his old lunch pail. It was far cooler than my square Batman and Robin lunchbox. Perhaps my admiration came from knowing Grandpa used it to carry his lunch daily to the shipyard. Or maybe it was just so different to this wide-eyed tyke compared to the standard superhero lunchboxes all my co-kindergartners carried. It was unconventional, it was weathered, it had history . . . it was my grandpa's.

That lunchbox and its contents contained my inheritance. An inheritance that was worthless, but priceless to me. An inheritance that sparked a fire that captivating my young mind, envisioning a world beyond Brownhelm. Inside Grandpa's pail was money, lots of it. Oodles of cash, but no greenbacks. Not a single portrait of Washington could be found. It had plenty of other colorful currency: lire, yen, francs, pounds, pesos, marks, drachmas, even rubles! These, to a Cold War kid, were pretty cool.

All that cash was from nations Dad had visited from his time at sea. I was fascinated by the different bills, the denominations in various widths and lengths, some quite wide, others not much bigger than a business card. All the different designs, timeworn and flushed with faded color. They were a slice of antiquity for my hungry eyes. To this pint-sized pirate, Grandpa's lunchbox was a treasure chest full of dollars from the World Bank of yesteryear. The lunchbox safeguarded the cash and coin collected by my father when he circumnavigated the globe before the age of twenty. I especially loved the bills that depicted kings and queens and military heroes in full regalia. They were works of art. At face value there was minimal monetary worth. Yet these weightless bills weighed heavily on my imagination and compounded my desire to see the world. Granddad's porcelain pail was a crystal ball to me. When I looked inside, I saw the riches of all those nations summoning me to a life of adventure and travel.

Dad's folks came from Budapest to the industrial boomtown of Cleveland, rich with all ethnicities from Eastern Europe. Dad was a twin in a family of three sons. After Dad's high-seas adventures, he returned to Ohio. With $2000, he brought a tractor-trailer rig and made local and regional runs transporting whatever needed to be moved. Be it car parts to and from Detroit, alkaline batteries to Chicago, clothes to West Virginia, or tires to Kentucky, Dad hauled it all. That lasted until he received a letter in the mail from a relative in Washington. Uncle Sam was writing him to go to Korea, 6,483 miles away. He was drafted into the drifts of the harsh winters on the front lines to fight communist aggression. In just two years he made the rank of Staff Seargent (E6). He was awarded the Bronze Star for his meritorious service in a combat zone. Like most who returned from war, Dad didn't talk about it, even when prodded.

After the war, Dad continued driving around the Buckeye State and beyond. Life for my mother was anything but a joyride. She was a single parent raising three kids from a previous marriage. She struggled to make ends meet to keep her children enrolled in Catholic school. Mom was born and raised in Providence. Her parents had arrived from Rome with three children and then had ten more. My mother was the twelfth of thirteen children. She migrated to the Midwest via the Navy, albeit indirectly.

She fell in love with a sailor named Paul Swartz. He was from Amherst, a neighboring town of Lorain. He was a few years older and a medic in the Pacific Campaign. After the war ended, he was stationed in Newport. Mom married him and, like her parents, got busy in the baby-making business. In five years, she gave birth to three children. Mom and Paul left the salt air of the East Coast for the pastures of the Heartland.

Paul was a hot-head who angered in an instant and liked the devil's juice, which turned him into an evil spirit. He was a small-town boy who was scarred from the big-time horrors of war. They didn't have a name for it then, but he suffered from PTSD. Relatives of both families say those two should have never gotten married.

Despite having a seven-, six-, and two-year-old with Paul Swartz, my mother filed for divorce. Mom never told her parents. Her mother, a hard-core Catholic, would have insisted she make it work, despite the fact that Paul had once, in an alcoholic rage, demanded Mom get on her knees and beg for her life while he held a meat cleaver over her head. Mom sweet-talked him, told him how much she loved him, how she adored him, that he was her everything. She told him, "You're tired. You need to relax. Let me get you a beer." He needed another beer like he needed another cleaver in his hand. But it worked. He passed out.

The abuse had been escalating. The cleaver was the final act of violence my mother would be subjected to. She had managed to sock some cash away and that night she fled and moved in with a girlfriend.

Mom was a tough one. She stood five-foot tall, but would flatten you verbally, and even physically if need be. She was proud of her *I don't take any nonsense from nobody* demeanor. She asked me once, "Do you know why I'm so tough?" Puzzled by the question and before I had time to answer, she said, "I get it from my mother." Grandma was 4'11" but ferocious as a lioness. Mom told the story about when she used to babysit for a Jewish couple, Harvey and Mona Gottlieb. They lived a couple of blocks away. They had two daughters, a four- and a five-year-old. Mom was twelve and they would pay her a quarter an hour to babysit. This was the late 1930s.

One day while babysitting, Mom was late for supper and her mother called the Gottliebs. Her mother asked when she would be home. Mom said she would be home in a little bit because she was doing the dishes.

The phone went dead. Mom thought she was going to be punished for being late for dinner.

Grandma slammed the phone. She flung open the door. She stormed out of the house, a crossfire hurricane. Anger spewed from her soul to her soles as she punished the sidewalk with every trounce. Arriving at the Gottliebs', she burst through the front door. Harvey, Mona, and their two daughters were having dinner as the fury of Mama Simonelli unleashed. The Gottliebs' domain was going to get rocked.

Grandma clamped Mona by her ear with a death grip and yanked her vertically out of the chair. She marched her to the kitchen sink where my mother stood, elbows deep in suds. With a handful of ear, Grandma locked Mona down face-to-face, inches away from her daughter. Her thick accent smeared over her thin knowledge of English. "Iza my daughta Rosa Carmella Simonelli, notta yo nigger."

Harvey was stunned, along with my mom and the

couple's two horrified girls.

Grandma grabbed my mom by her wet hand and exited like the crack of a lightning strike as the Gottlieb residence smoldered in her wrath. That wasn't toughness. That was more like terrorism. I don't condone the use of the N-word. In fact, I vehemently condemn it.

That's why my mom was ferociously tough: it was inherited. It was a different era; you had to be tough, especially if you were an immigrant. It wasn't only inherited through DNA. It was societal. Like her mother, Mom developed into a lioness with an animal-kingdom mentality: survival of the fittest, don't take any nonsense from anyone, and stick up for yourself. The Italians and Irish were considered the scourge of immigrants. The WOPS and Micks, as they were called, were not well-received. Actually, all undocumented foreigners during the Great Wave of Immigration were known as WOPS. It was an acronym for *without papers*. For whatever reason, it stuck to the Italians like mozzarella on pizza, and Mom would flatten anybody who even thought of calling her that.

Intent on keeping her children enrolled in Catholic school, she worked three jobs. Life before Mom met my dad was anything but a joyride. This was the early 1950s. Living in the projects, she cleaned homes and was a cashier at Meyer Goldberg, the local supermarket, but her main source of income was as a waitress at the Hollywood Bar on Elyria Ave in Lorain. That brought cash in every night. The HB, as it was known by locals, was also a restaurant, conveniently situated within crawling distance from Dad's house. HB was his watering hole; he was frequently there with his best friend, Arthur. On one of those visits, Otto met Rosie. Dad, twenty-six, fresh from the front lines of Korea, was looking to settle down. Find a bride for life's ride.

Dad took a fancy to a particular waitress. What began as drinking drafts and snacking on Beer Nuts at the bar shifted to dinner and beer in a booth. Dad never was much of a cook and the HB served as his eatery of choice with his newfound friendship with that waitress.

I asked him, "What was the draw, the attraction?" He laughed, paused, reflected. All the while his blue eyes shimmered with his love for her. "She was a good-looking broad." I love that term *broad*, in a Frank Sinatra, Humphrey Bogart way. A very midcentury term which my father still uses as a catchall. Young broad, old broad, crazy broad, funny broad, smart broad . . . that is Dad's universal word for the opposite sex. "And . . . she was a great waitress." He beamed as he told me, "HB would get packed on Friday and Saturday nights. Your mother was all over that place taking orders, serving, clearing tables, lighting guest's cigarettes. Sometimes she would go behind the bar and serve drinks. I always sat in her area. She was something to watch, always on the rush, *go, go, go* and everybody liked her. Seemed like she knew what you wanted before you knew. (That would explain her self-professed psychic abilities.)

"After a month or two, I asked her out. She said, 'Get the frig outta here. I got three kids.'" Dad's comeback was heroic. He said, "I'll love them, too." Dad launched cupid's flaming arrow, piercing her cold heart, still icy toward men because of a failed marriage. Dad's line was the icebreaker. Even so, he had to chip away. Mom was no pushover. After continually rejecting Dad's requests to go out, Arthur stepped in, singing Dad's praises. He told my mom that Dad was crazy about her. They ended up dating for about two years and were married unceremoniously by the JOP at City Hall. I always enjoyed Mom's version. "There was your father, skinny, all one-hundred-nineteen pounds of him. I coulda knocked him over in one breath. He would guzzle that beer out of the bottle, *gug, gug, gug,*" she said, imitating the chugging sounds. "His Adam's apple would go up and down. It was the cutest thing." She lit up like a little girl blushing from a school-boy crush. Attraction is indeed a funny thing, and the story always made me smile when she told it.

Dad punched the clock every day at the Ford Motor Company Lorain Assembly Plant for thirty years. He loved his job. It was a short commute from home. The Plant, as he called it, was less than three miles from our house. Every day, without fail, before he left for work he would hug and kiss my mother and say, "I love you, dear," or use some other endearment such as sweetie, honey, or Rosie. My mom would follow suit, saying, "I love you dear", or perhaps it was baby, or Otts." Ott, or Otts, was a nickname my mom and good friends of my dad used. I have inherited that nickname from family and only my dearest of friends.

When those parting words left my parents' lips, they gazed into each other's eyes with a passion redolent of teenage lust. When my parents kissed, the whole universe stopped. You could sense it; you could feel it. I lived it and was blessed to experience it every day while living under their roof. There was no doubt this was the house that love built. My dad would grab his pressed aluminum lunchbox and head out the door to make the short drive to the plant. As he would pull out of the driveway, my mother would take the position she did every day, planting herself at the living room window facing west onto Sunnyside Road. She'd pull the curtain back to peer out. Dad would hang a left and head south, driving as slow as a senior citizen. He would honk the horn and wave and Mom would wave back. Dad would come to a complete halt at the four-way intersection of Cooper Foster and Sunnyside, giving Mom enough time to bop from the front window to the large nine-panel bay window that faced south. Pulling the chocolate brown drapery back, it was honk, wave, repeat. This ritual of Mom and Dad's took place daily. This was . . . love.

One day in my later years, I was home visiting them for a few days. I was walking down the hallway and heard a commotion and laughter. At first it caught me off guard. I didn't know where it was coming from. Then I realized the source was the master bedroom. It was my parental units getting busy. No son or daughter wants to hear or see their parents doing the wild thing. Like a train wreck, I stopped to gawk. There was nothing to see beyond the beige walls, nor did I want to. Yet the audio was loud and clear. I heard, "Is that the stick shift or the ball bearings?"

"What do you think, Rosie?" was big Otto's reply.

I snickered silently. Mom and Dad, two old lovebirds were cooing in their nest. My parents were robust between the sheets well into their sixties. I walked away that day, charmed by fairytale love, knowing they were having fun, loving each other, taking each other for a test drive as if it was the first time. We should all be so blessed.

My father adored my mother. My mother cherished my father. My parents were deeply in love and it showed for nearly fifty years. They did everything together in a perfect picture of unconditional love. Mom said, "Marriage isn't always fifty-fifty, sometimes it's ninety-ten. Sometimes you have the ninety, sometimes you have the ten. But you always have to give it 100%." That's why their marriage was successful—they worked on being 100% one-hundred percent of the time.

My parents weren't perfect, nor was their marriage, but they were perfect together. To this day, in my own relationships, in all my worldly travels, I have rarely discovered the unique, uncompromising, and unconditional love Mom and Dad shared. It is paradise to have such an emotion for one human being and in return receive that love. David Viscott penned,

"To love and be loved is to feel the sun from both sides." That was my mom and my dad, perpetually gleaming rays of sunshine, nestled in a glow of 24/7 warmth. I long for the day to find a lady that will travel with me, beaming from the other side of sun where my parents lived, loved, and prospered.

■

Your children are not your children. They are the sons and daughters of life's longing for itself. They come through you but not from you, and though they are with you, yet they belong not to you. You might give them your love but not your thoughts for they have their own thoughts.

KAHLIL GIBRAN, THE PROPHET

There be three things which are too wonderful for me,
yea, four which I know not:
The way of an eagle in the air;
the way of a serpent upon a rock;
the way of a ship in the midst of the sea;
and the way of a man with a maid.

PROVERBS 30:18-19

■

LEMON MERINGUE PIE

THIS WAS MOM'S FAVORITE, period. I occasionally made it on Mother's Day or her birthday, or whenever it struck my fancy. I don't know why, but Mom always called this an old ladies' dessert.

One prebaked 9-inch pie shell, chilled,
or scratch made crust preferred

FILLING

1 cup water

1 cup sugar, more or less, depending how sweet or tart
you like the lemon filling

Pinch of salt

½ cup lemon juice

2 lemons, zested

⅓ cup cornstarch

4 egg yolks, reserve whites for meringue

4 tablespoons sweet butter

MERINGUE

4 egg whites

½ – ¾ cup sugar

Combine water, sugar, salt, lemon juice, and zest and bring to a boil. Beat the yolks well, add the cornstarch and mix until blended thoroughly. Once the liquid has come to a boil, temper some of the hot liquid into the cornstarch yolk mixture.

Once the mixture has been tempered, with the lemon water boiling, whisk in the egg cornstarch mixture and cook until thickened. Remove from heat and stir in butter until melted and incorporated. Pour into the pre-baked pie shell and let stand at room temperature, then refrigerate until it is solidified.

Place the whites in a clean mixing bowl with the sugar and whip until a stiff peak is achieved. You can use a spatula or palette knife to apply the meringue. For a fancy effect, pipe the meringue with a pastry bag. Dust the top with powdered sugar and brown in a 425° oven. Or simply brown with a hand-held torch available at restaurant supply stores or kitchen specialty shops.

Taste the Freedom.

CHAPTER 5

1,036 DAYS

MUSICAL PAIRING: Goes great with "Chimes of Freedom"
BOB DYLAN, VINTAGE, 1964

WAS A MERE FIVE MONTHS OLD when Senator John F. Kennedy kissed my cheek. Of course, I don't remember. But Mom ensured I never forgot that significant smooch. Nor did she let anyone else forget the day she met the future President of the United States. Like many people in 1960, especially the female populace, my mom was Kennedy crazy. With good reason: he was rugged, handsome, Harvard educated, a Navy hero, articulate, charismatic, natty, classy, and wealthy. The cherry on the cake for Mom: she was from Providence and JFK was from Boston, an hour away, and they were both Catholic. In her world, that classified her and Jack Kennedy as neighbors, and nobody could dare tell her otherwise.

"Your mom was nuts about him," Dad told me.

JFK arrived in the blue-collar town of Lorain, Ohio on September 27, 1960. The industrial municipality, rich with over seventy different ethnicities, is simply known as the International City. The faithful masses packed George Daniel Field on that Indian summer day to hear the future Commander in Chief deliver his speech about the New Frontier, the centerpiece to his campaign. He spoke with vigor, imagination and foresight. It was a big deal. It was the first time in the history of Lorain a presidential nominee had campaigned there. The city of 70,000 came out in full force, including JFK's neighbor, my mother.

As I write this fifty-five years later, I wonder why mom took me, and only me, just months old, to the political rally. She could have taken any one of my three brothers, or my sister, or all of us for that matter. Back in those days, politicians really did kiss babies. Perhaps she thought bringing me would create an opportunity for her to meet Kennedy. Whether intentional or not, Mom was determined to meet her neighbor.

JFK was born in 1917 and was the first president born in the 20th century to be elected president in the same century. This represented a new way of thinking, a far more progressive mentality than that of presidents of another era.

He conveyed inspiration encouraging the blue-collar crowd to think beyond the smoke-stack skyline of Lorain, all the way through to amber waves of grain and far beyond.

JFK envisioned an invisible bridge with the global citizenry serving as the construction crew; humans becoming the bolts in that bridge, supporting one another, responsible for maintaining hope and freedom throughout the world . . . a freedom for all people of all ethnicities. He believed that, despite our differences politically, socially, economically, and religiously, we all belong to the same tribe: the human race. He believed that freedom is not just a way of life, it is the only way. He challenged the crowd to each look outside themselves and, in turn, to collectively answer the higher call of duty—to their country, to the world. He believed in lifting yourself so others would be lifted in the process.

As he finished his speech to hearty applause, the crowd began to exit. Mom started walking back to the station wagon, pushing me ahead of her in the stroller. On the way to the car she encountered a crowd of people standing in a makeshift line underneath the bleachers. My mother, never shy, asked why they were standing there. When she told the story, she says she thought they were handing out campaign buttons. She wanted one of those *All the Way with JFK buttons*. To her surprise, someone in the group said, "Senator Kennedy is coming." That's all Mom needed to hear. I wouldn't be a bit surprised if, after applying the brake on the baby stroller's wheels, she opened her purse and pulled out her compact to check her hair and lipstick. Don't all women do that when meeting their presidential nominee neighbor?

Within minutes, several thin men with thinner ties,

clothed in stern black suits, were asking people to form a single line, then aligned themselves to face the onlookers. "Here he comes!" A jubilant voice rose from the far end of the line. I am sure when she heard that, her endorphins began to combust like firecrackers on Chinese New Year. There he was, the man who would be president: John Fitzgerald Kennedy. As he made his way through the line, he edged closer to her. At that moment she decided to unlock the stroller and put it behind her to give herself unobstructed access to the handsome candidate. Removing me from the stroller and holding me over her left shoulder, Mom was now in visible contact with JFK. Just a few more hands to shake and she would be face to face with the man she so adored.

"Hello, how are you?" JFK asked Mom.

"Fine," she replied, at a loss for words, captivated by his magnetism. Intuitively following custom, she and JFK knew what to do. For that split second in time they were doing the campaign dance, also known as meet, greet, grin and grip, or press the flesh. Mom turned me from the nestled position on her shoulder and brought me front and center. That's when JFK leaned forward and pecked my cheek, then proceeded moving down the line of well-wishers.

"It happened so quick . . . and boy is he handsome . . . and he kissed Junior!" Mom would gush to anyone who would listen. I am not certain whether she was happier about meeting JFK, or the fact that he planted a kiss on my cheek. Although just months old, I was present for one of my mother's most cherished moments and eternally a part of the favorite story in her life.

Something supernatural happened that day, a metaphysical experience, if you will. A flash encounter with a visionary leader. I do not believe in coincidence, unless of course it is divine coincidence. In that bright shining celestial nanosecond, the incomprehensible laws of the universe synthesized two spirits together, young and old for reasons perhaps only known by mystics.

JFK went on to win the election, becoming the thirty-fifth president, at forty-three years young, the youngest president ever elected. Historical notes of his presidency include the Cuban Missile Crisis, the Bay of Pigs, creation of the Peace Corp, and, most notable, his vision to expand NASA, and in so doing, challenging America to land a man on the moon and return him safely to Earth before the end of the decade.

In step with his call to action, a new generation accepted his charge to illuminate the world with goodwill, hope, and the promise of a better tomorrow for all.

He was the first celebrity president and, along with his wife, Jaqueline, they became the first and ultimate power couple. I don't think any other president and first lady, before or since, has had the class, charm, grace and elegance as Jack and Jackie.

During his presidency, they were they most popular people in the world. JFK was a man who called the shots, right on down to the selection of who would play him in the movie PT 109. First Lady Jaqueline wanted Warren Beatty. Jack wanted Cliff Robertson. Jack got his way. While he handled domestic and international policy issues, Jaqueline refurbished the White House, expanding and celebrating the arts and humanities.

On Valentine's Day 1962, CBS aired *A Tour of the White House*. It was exceedingly popular, given Jacqueline Kennedy's celebrity status. The documentary was made available to 106 countries—half the world! At the Emmys later that year, she was presented a special Academy of Television Arts and Sciences Trustees Award for the White House tour documentary. In the most organic way, the world fell in love with her. With that love affair, the negative attention upon her husband diminished. As JFK was thrust front and center in the Cold War, the First Lady quietly went to work behind the scenes. She was the softness to his rough edges, gathering global attention. Her brains and beauty wooed international dignitaries and heads of state, thus making friends for her husband's opposition to the spread of communism. Multilingual, an accomplished equestrian, a photo journalist, protector of American art and antiquities, and easy on the eyes, it's no secret this fashion icon was the secret weapon in the Kennedy administration.

She was responsible for hiring René Verdon who had been employed at La Caravelle, the temple of haute cuisine in Manhattan. René bought a level of sophisticated cuisine never seen before in the White House. In the past, the food had been prepared by Navy cooks or outside catering firms that crafted food that was average at best. Taking his visionary cue from JFK, Verdon grew herbs on the grounds and brought haute cuisine to new heights—literally. He grew vegetables on the roof.

Verdon insisted on local and seasonal foods well before farm-to-table became the muddied verbiage it is today. Although he does not get the credit he deserves, hand in hand with the First Lady, America turned its tummy to all things French. In tandem, they raised the level of sophisticated cuisine and dining in America. His cultural impact, the rapid evolution of American gastronomy, began with him at 1600 Pennsylvania Avenue in 1961.

Some culinary archivists state the Kennedy era officially ended in 1966 when Verdon resigned during the Johnson Administration. The Johnsons brought in a budget-minded bean counter who insisted on frozen and canned vegetables. They wanted BBQ, beans, and cornbread, a culinary conflict from the Kennedy sophistication of chateaubriand and crêpessuzette. Verdon was quite vocal about the Johnsons' food choices. He once told the *Washington Post,* "You can eat at home what you want, but you do not serve barbecued spareribs at a banquet with ladies in white gloves." He left the White House in a huff, stating "I do not want to lose my reputation." Continuing, "It was very lousy to serve frozen food in the presidents house.

The era of Camelot began officially on November 29,

1963, exactly one week after Jack Kennedy's assassination. Jacqueline Kennedy had contacted Theodore H. White, a reporter for *Life* magazine and implored him to write these words about her husband. She was so young, only thirty-four when she sat in the back seat of the Lincoln convertible, her pink Chanel dress bloodied from her husband's brains in her lap. She recounted the story to White of what had happened just one week ago, as calm and stoic as her husband had always been, insistent that Jack be remembered as a hero. She spoke of the Arthurian legend of *Camelot*, a Broadway musical he loved, written by Alan Jay Lerner, a classmate of Kennedy's at Harvard. The soundtrack was favored bedtime music in the White House.

JFK's favorite line came in the last song, when King Arthur knighted a young boy. The new knight is instructed by the king to tell the story of Camelot to future generations.

Don't let it be forgot
That once there was a spot
For one brief, shining moment
That was known as Camelot[1]

Jaqueline recited that line to White, then added, "There will be great presidents again, but there will never be another Camelot."

---

1 Verses from **CAMELOT**, a copyrighted musical by Alan Jay Lerner (book and lyrics) and Frederick Loewe (music), based on the King Arthur legend as adapted from the 1958 T. H. (Terence Hanbury) White novel, *The Once and Future King*. The play premiered on Broadway from December 3, 1960 (a month after JFK won the Presidency) and closed on January 5, 1963.

Given the state of affairs, it's astonishing how she maintained the composure to create the legacy of Camelot. This proclamation curbed negative press about JFK and his legacy. It uplifted a nation that was grieving right alongside her. She truly believed JFK was magic and ensured his enchantment would live in eternity. No other First Lady had the panache or savoir faire she radiated. She elevated her role to popstar status and iconic trendsetter, winning the hearts and minds of the admiring world around her. Not one president, ever, has been given a moniker so fitting as that of Camelot.

Perhaps JFK was so ambitious and visionary because he was predisposed to believe he would die at a young age. He had, in fact, predicted he would die by age forty-five. He was off by just six months. His morbid premonitions were exemplified with his favorite poem, "I Have a Rendezvous with Death" by Alan Seeger. He was no stranger to death: his oldest brother Joe Jr. was killed over the English Channel after volunteering for a top-secret mission on August 12, 1944, just two days before the end of the war, and his sister, Kathleen, died in a plane crash over France in 1948. Another sister, Rosemary, was institutionalized in 1941 after a failed lobotomy and was ostracized from the family. He and Jacqueline endured the heartache of losing two children. A daughter, Arabella, was stillborn in August 1956. A son, Patrick, died in August 1963 within thirty-six hours of being born.

He was surrounded by death and misfortune—some call it the Kennedy curse—and escaped his own trio of near-death experiences, each time being given last rites. In 1947, he became gravely ill while visiting England. In 1951, while in Japan, he had a fever so high it nearly killed him. Then in 1954, after back surgery, he contracted a staph infection that left him comatose for weeks.

Perhaps these close calls and an intimate association with death gave him an elevated appreciation for living. His lust for life was well-documented, his unscrupulous behavior nautical miles away from that of an officer and a gentleman. Kennedy believed time was his enemy. That belief transformed him into the patron saint of risky behavior. Yes, he was flawed, like so many great leaders before him: Jefferson, Lincoln, Churchill. Yet he was tested by the fire of personal hardship and tragic circumstance. From an inferno of life's tragedies emerged a courageous, compassionate, tolerant visionary who desired freedom for the world.

That was the magic of JFK. Yes, he was a flawed warrior from a connected multi-millionaire family. A man who had already been rejected as 4-F for a bad back, ulcers, and asthma, who later obtained a falsified physical just so he could enlist in the Navy. Certainly, he was guided by his father, who told him, "If you are going to be in public service you must enter the war." God doesn't call the qualified, He qualifies the call.

Heroes are birthed in the horror of war. On the evening of August 1, 1943, Lieutenant Kennedy and his twelve shipmates on PT-109 patrolled waters near the Solomon Islands, looking for enemy ships. It was a cloudy, moonless night. Around 2:30 a.m., the 400-foot Japanese destroyer, *Amagiri*, rammed the 80-foot wood-hulled PT boat, slicing it in half. Most of the crew flew into the fiery water, while Kennedy ricocheted inside the cockpit, further damaging his back. Two shipmates perished, most likely from the impact, and a third, badly wounded by exploding fuel, was incapable of swimming—seventy-percent of his body had been burned. Kennedy. who had competed on Harvard's swim team, took to the ocean like a dolphin. Between his teeth he clamped the strap of the burned man's life-vest, then headed for the nearest island not under Japanese control. It took four hours for Kennedy and crew to swim the three-and-a-half miles.

The island was 100 yards in diameter, with no food and no water. On August 4, they swam four miles toward the desolate micro-island of Olasana. But that island had no fresh water either, and for food Kennedy and crew relied on coconuts and rainwater caught in leaves. On August 5, two aboriginal men arrived in an outrigger canoe. They were islander scouts for the Allies.

Kennedy, at the suggestion of a tribesman, carved a message on a coconut husk with his knife, with hopes the scouts could get it to the Aussies. It read in capital letters:
NAURO ISL
COMMANDER... NATIVE KNOWS
POS'IT ... HE CAN PILOT ... 11 ALIVE
NEED SMALL BOAT ... KENNEDY

The crew of PT-109 was rescued August 8.

JFK received the Navy and Marine Corps Medal for heroism, and a Purple Heart for battle wounds. He saved the coconut, had it encased in plastic, then inset it onto a circular wooden base. It served as a paperweight on his desk in the Oval Office, a daily reminder of quick thinking and his crew. In a strange twist of fate, Lieutenant Commander Kohei Hanami, who had commanded the *Amagiri*, attended Kennedy's inauguration in 1961.

How a man unfit for military service joined the Navy, commanded a PT boat, and became a hero is the stuff of legend. In an interview, when asked how he became a war hero, Kennedy replied, "It was involuntary. They sank my boat."

His charisma, his innate inspirational capabilities, catapulted him to become one of the greatest—if not *the* greatest—leaders in American history. Good leaders enable their followers to believe in their leadership. Great leaders inspire people to believe in themselves. I still remain inspired by the thirty-fifth President of the United States.

I leave you with words that were never spoken. This is an excerpt from a speech he was to give on the evening of November 22, 1963, to the Texas State Democratic Committee, in Municipal Auditorium in Austin. JFK was assassinated in Dallas, earlier that same day.

My greatest hope is that a future president is reading these words. That he or she will not merely take a page out of the Kennedy playbook, but seize the whole playbook with confident hands and run with it, inspiring us to believe in ourselves, our leaders, our nation, and the world.

> "... *for this country is moving, and it must not stop. It cannot stop. For this is a time for courage and a time for challenge. Neither conformity nor complacency will do. Neither the fanatics nor the fainthearted are needed. And our duty as a party is not to our party alone, but to the nation and, indeed, to all mankind. Our duty is not merely the preservation of political power but the preservation of peace and freedom.*
>
> *"So, let us not be petty when our cause is so great. Let us not quarrel amongst ourselves when our nation's future is at stake. Let us stand together with renewed confidence in our cause— united in our heritage of the past and our hopes for the future—and determined that this land we love shall lead all mankind into new frontiers of peace and abundance."*

■

The true hero is flawed.
The true test of a champion
is not whether he can triumph,
but whether he can overcome obstacles
—preferably of his own making—
in order to triumph."

GARTH STEIN

Where there is no vision, the people perish.

PROVERBS 29:18

■

NEW ENGLAND CLAM CHOWDER
SOUTH OF BOSTON STYLE

From the *White House Chef Cook Book* by René Verdon. This was JFK's favorite, and it is reported that one time he asked for it three days in row.

4 dozen medium-size clams

5 cups cold water[1]

1 two-inch piece of salt pork, diced

1 large onion, chopped very fine

4 medium potatoes, diced

2 cups milk, hot

1½ cups heavy cream, hot

Salt and pepper to taste

Wash the clams thoroughly and place them in a deep pan with cold water. Bring to a boil and cook for about ten minutes or until the clams open. Strain the broth through a chinois or cheesecloth; reserve. Remove the clams from the shell and rough chop. Combine salt pork and onion in saucepan and cook gently over low heat about 5 minutes—do not brown. Add reserved broth, potatoes, salt, and pepper. Cook until potatoes are tender. Add milk and cream, bring to a boil, add the clams. Serve immediately.

Yields 8-10 servings

Taste the Freedom.

1   I suggest using fish stock instead of water, or supplement some of the water with clam juice, which you can purchase at grocery stores. Also, a thickener, such as a roux or cornstarch, will give the chowder added body. You may also use diced bacon instead of salt pork.

CHAPTER 6

GET A LEG UP

MUSICAL PAIRING: Goes great with "I Won't Back Down"
TOM PETTY, VINTAGE 1989

"YOU BETTER TAKE JUNIOR to the doctor," Dad instructed Mom. It was September 1966 and although it happened over half a century ago, I remember it like yesterday. I had made the jump from kindergarten to first grade at Brownhelm Elementary. I was a big boy now: first grade! Despite my excitement, after the first week I limped my way to the school bus, to class, to recess, back to class, and back home. My mother thought the brand-new back-to-school shoes were too tight. Yet my feet never hurt. As a matter of fact, nothing hurt, not even slightly. This confounded my parents.

Dad called me close to him and proceeded to do a little parental checkup from toe to thigh. I removed my sock and shoe from the left leg. I stood upon my right leg as my father sat in front of me with my foot in his hands. Guiding my foot upward and downward, left to right, he asked, "Does it hurt?" It didn't. With my foot in his lap he jostled my ankle then went northward, squeezing my shin and calf muscle, still asking, "Does this hurt?" The answer remained the same. He poked and prodded, twisting, thumping and testing every which way.

"You didn't know Dad was a doctor, did you?" said Mom.

Dad gave me a quick karate chop below the knee. I laughed as my lower leg jerked forward, passing the reflex test.

"I don't know, Rosie," was Dr. Dad's prognosis.

"Maybe he's got a charley horse."

"No, he'd be in pain, and he's not in pain. I didn't feel any knots or tightness."

"What's a charley horse? Do you get it from riding horses?" I asked, bringing a snicker from my parents. It made sense to ask; there were horses all around Brownhelm.

"Let's see what the doctor has to say about this," Dad said.

Off to Dr Haley we went the next day.

■

Mom sat in the examination room with me.

"What is the problem with little Otto, Mrs. Borsich?" the bespectacled, black-haired doc asked.

"He has been walking with a limp the past few days. We thought it would go away, but it hasn't."

"How do you feel, young man? Any pain anywhere?"

When I told him "no", he instructed me to head into the hallway and walk from one end to the other. Back in the examination room, he gave me the same kind of inspection I'd gotten from Dad.

"Mrs. Borsich, I don't know what is causing your son to limp. The good news is, he is not in any pain. His foot, ankle, and knee joints are functional, and I did not detect any bumps or lumps. I suggest you take him to the hospital and get an X-ray because there's something going on that we cannot see."

With a grape sucker in my hand, we left the doctor's and headed home.

The next day after school Mom picked me up and we went directly to the St Joseph's emergency room for my nonemergency. After a long wait, someone called my name. I spun around, and there was a nurse with a clipboard just a few feet away. She looked angelic in all white: shoes, chalky hose, knee-length skirt and the customary snow white, starched hat. Hers had a blue band. The sharp angle of the back of the hat reminded me of a Cadillac with big fins.

Mom and I followed the nurse into the bank of emergency rooms, all separated by long thin melon-green curtains. The nurse grabbed the curtain and walked it around, enclosing us from the rest of the beds. "You can put your son up here," she said, tapping the bed. I hopped up, crinkling the paper sheet beneath me.

"It says here you have a limp." Mom spoke up, bringing the nurse up to speed on the doctor's visit and the need for an X-ray. She began the mandatory checking of my vitals.

Swish, the curtain was drawn back and there stood a tall older man, balding with thin white hair. He was animated. "I'm Doctor Cummings" he addressed us while grabbing the chart. "Young man, it says here you are limping with no known cause or injury?"

"Yep."

"How long have you been limping?"

"About five days," Mom interjected.

"You are not in any pain?"

"Nope."

"Were you ever in any pain?"

"Nope."

"And you have been checked out by your family physician and he sent you here, recommending an X-ray?"

"Yes."

"Well that's what we shall do. Okay, young man, are you ready to go for a ride?"

"Yes!" I didn't know what kind of ride he had in mind, but I was ready."

"Have a seat back on the bed and a nurse will be here to take you to X-ray."

Zooming in the wheel chair we went. Arriving at the

X-ray waiting room, we were greeted by a female X-ray tech. She wheeled me into the X-ray room.

Grabbing a couple of lead sheets the size of a legal pad, she placed one across my upper thigh just below the pelvic region and another one just above my waist. For good measure she laid one atop my underwear to protect the family jewels, to minimize exposure to radiation. She stretched to grab the ceiling-mounted camera and positioned it between the two lead plates. Pointed directly at my pelvis, mere inches separated my flesh from the lens. She went behind a large wall which had a small window the size of an index card to peer out.

From beyond the barrier she said, "I'm going to count to three. When I say *three* I want you to hold your breath, okay?"

"Okay." When she said *two* I took a big inhale and locked my lungs.

"Three."

I was already holding my breath. I heard a click, a hum, and then a click again.

The tech appeared from behind the barrier. "Good job!" She adjusted the plates to continue taking photos of my knee, ankle, and foot. Planted in the wheelchair, I headed back to the ER to await the X-rays. Dr. Cummings sat us down in front of the bright white light to discuss the X-rays.

"There is nothing here out of the ordinary. All the bones are aligned properly. There are no chips or small fractures in any of the bones. These X-rays do not provide any information about why your son has developed a limp. My best advice is to make an appointment at the Cleveland Clinic. They have specialists who will determine what is causing your son to limp."

The Cleveland Clinic is consistently rated as one of the best hospitals, if not *the* best, in the world. Fortunately, it was a mere thirty miles due east as the crow flies from Brownhelm. It's comforting to have the best hospital in the world in your backyard. We saw Dr. Sphere, a pediatrician. He was a Lithuanian immigrant, short, balding, with a light brown complexion, and wearing glasses. He spoke with a slight accent. He knew his bones. After a look at the X-rays he made quick work on the diagnosis and prognosis and delivered the news. "Your son has Legg Perthes," said the doc.

Its full name is Legg–Calvé–Perthes disease, LCPD, or Perthes disease, named after the orthopedic surgeons who identified the childhood disease, Arthur Legg, Jacques Calvé and Georg Perthes. While this trio of specialists had their own theories of what causes Perthes disease, to this day the cause is not known. Medical professionals are, however, all in agreement there is a loss of blood flow from the femoral artery to the femoral or the femur—the upper-most part of the thigh bone that is rounded and fits into the pelvis, sometimes called the ball and socket joint. The restriction of blood prohibits the full development of the femur. It is difficult to identify Perthes because the only symptom is a limp from an unknown cause. Going unchecked, it will cause permanent deformity to the femur and is a sure-fire path to osteoarthritis. It is most common among children between four and eight.

There was a negligible flatness revealed on the X-ray that Dr. Cummings had overlooked. Dr. Sphere pulled out a pen from his lab coat. Using it as a pointer, he made a back-and-forth motion on the X-ray, emphasizing the imperfect arch of my femur as he explained to my parents that the loss of blood flow had restricted the development of the femur. "Your son will need to be placed in traction at the hospital," he said.

"For how long?" Mom asked.

"Well, as long as it takes. It could be anywhere from six to eight months to a year."

I heard *hospital for a year,* and began to flood the office with tears.

Dr. Sphere crouched down, level with my drowning eyes. "You are going to be fine. You are limping now, and we are going to fix that limp. You don't want to limp anymore, right?"

Sniffling, I just nodded.

Using his hands to demonstrate, he delivered a basic explanation to me. With one hand open, fingers spread wide and arched as if he were gripping a softball, with his opposite hand he made a tight fist. "This is your leg bone" he said, describing the fisted hand. "This is the pelvis," he said, emphasizing his clawed hand. Putting his fist inside the claw, he told me, "Your leg bone goes into the pelvis. They must fit like this, so you can walk or run. Your leg bone is a little flat." He removed his fist, opening it to create a more linear surface. "Your leg bone is sick, and we are going to make it better." As he demonstrated, trying to cup the flat hand, he said, "It's not fitting like it should, so you can run and jump. You want to run and jump, don't you?"

Still sniveling, I told him, "Yes." Dr. Sphere's explanation made perfect sense. He not only came down to my level, he explained everything in the most rudimentary way, so my boyhood brain could wrap my thoughts around it.

The next day I was admitted to St. Joseph's Hospital. Once I was on the bed, the nurses went to work. One of them at the head of the bed explained about the traction, telling me they were going to put a weight on my foot, but it wasn't going to hurt. "The most important thing," the nurse said, "is you have to lay down at all times. The only time you may sit up is when you go to the bathroom and when you are eating. You have to lay flat, so your leg will get better, okay?"

"Okay."

Two other nurses were working on my left leg as Mom and Dad looked on. One nurse grabbed a green roll off the cart. It was padding, about four inches wide, and perforated. It was thin, maybe an eighth of an inch. The nurse placed the roll midway on the outer side of my left calf. Then she unwound the roll downward toward my foot and across my heel, leaving a little slack or a loop, then continued padding up along my inner calf. As one nurse held the padding in place, the other nurse began to wrap an ACE bandage to secure the padding from the top, going around and around downward to my ankle, encasing the padding with the bandage. She placed two metal fasteners on it to secure the wrap.

Mom's and Dad's watchful eyes took it all in. The nurse nearest me said, "We're going to put a weight on your foot now. We need to pull your leg bone away, so it can heal. It's not going to hurt one bit." A nurse at the foot of the bed grabbed a black metal V-shaped device. The nurse latched the V onto the green fabric loop at the base of my foot. Then, grabbing a nylon line, she fastened it to the V. At the other end of the line was a fifteen-pound weight aided by a pulley. This was traction. The nurse was right. It didn't hurt one bit. So began the treatment. The purpose was to separate the femur from the pelvis and prohibit any excess wear and tear that could potentially cause irreparable damage. The femur had to revascularize. Meaning, the blood vessels had to extend to the femur for it to regenerate itself.

That was my life at age six. In the hospital, flat on my back, a fifteen-pound weight pulling my leg out of socket. Days turned into weeks as the Indian summer faded. I watched the trees from my fourth-floor window. They morphed from green to gold. The aroma of fall was in the air, yet my room reeked of antibacterial agents. I could only dream of the frost on the pumpkin from my cold hospital room. There would be no jack-o'-lanterns or bobbing for apples. Mom brought me her famous apple spice cake, my favorite. The warm spices were comforting, reminding me of someplace I had not been in a while—home—where that cake should have been enjoyed with family, not in a disinfected hospital room. However, I was thrilled Mom brought a little slice of happiness to the hospital to indulge my senses.

My parents had a discussion with Dr. Sphere and Dr. Dad prescribed a home remedy. He suggested and convinced Dr. Sphere to release me from the hospital prior to the completion of traction. He presented his point of view to the doctor and it was crystal clear. After nearly three months in the hospital I was going home! I am not sure who was happier, Mom and Dad, or me.

We lived in a modest home. Six children in a four-bedroom, one-bath house. The house was heated by an oil-burning furnace. The room where the furnace was, was simply known as the furnace room. That became my bedroom, my at-home hospital room. I was now in traction at home. That fifteen-pound weight from St Joseph's was now in my possession. Attached via the green foam and ACE bandage, it hung over the foot of the bed.

That room also became the TV room. My parents decided to move the black and white console into the furnace room so I could watch TV. They didn't have to do that, but nightly, the furnace room, my bedroom, served as a primitive precursor to today's media room. The whole family sacrificed in some way during my bedridden days. Dad affixed a table on the wall. It had a hinge that would enable it to be raised or lowered with a nylon strand. He even drilled a large hole in the upper-right corner to serve as a cup holder. That folding counter served as my kitchen table. It's where I ate Mom's good cooking. Every day I had breakfast in bed, as well as lunch and dinner.

I didn't go to school; school came to me in the form of Mrs. Fowell. She had jet-black hair, pulled back, and was simple in dress and style, but commanding in her teaching skills. She was my tutor, a definitive schoolmarm. She was strict. Her first order of business was to inform my mom to remove the TV. "That television is not conducive to your son's education," she told my mom in front me. "It's a distraction to the educational process."

"The family comes in here to watch TV," said Mom.

"Where was the TV before Otto came home?"

"In the living room."

"Then I suggest you put it back there."

With the TV gone, I dreamed. I dreamed of adventure, of faraway lands. I gazed out of the lone curtainless window every day. Eyes focused beyond vastness, planning my escape from that medically prescribed ball and chain anchored around my left leg. I fantasized of life beyond that furnace room and catching fire with a life of my own. My imagination was crackling with intensity, an inferno burning through every nook and cranny of my cranium. I was born a dreamer, and no Perthes disease, no tough tutor, no removal of TV, would ever keep me down.

That was my life for ten months. Eat, tutor, study, dream, sleep, repeat. Every month Mom would take me to St Joseph's. I was nearly on a first-name basis with some of the staff there. Especially the X-ray techs. It was necessary to get X-rayed monthly to check on the progress of the traction and to monitor just how far the femur had become dislodged.

Usually it was just Mom and me. Almost always there was a treat involved after the radioactive photoshoot. Despite traction, I could walk, though that was only allowed once a month. During that precious reprieve, I'd walk in Lakewood Park on the shores of Lake Erie to watch the boats go by, take a trip to Mill Hollow, the nearby park to feed the ducks, or have a double-dip crunch cone from Dairy Queen. I realize how special those times were. I was laid up for a wearisome amount of time. My only outdoor activity was the ride to the hospital. Mom ensured if I was going to be outside, it was best to make a day of it and she made those trips special for me. I was able to walk under my own power, but my limp became notably worse. Dr. Sphere commented that despite the increased limping, the traction was making progress. The ball and socket joint were being extricated from each other—exactly like he had demonstrated.

"We are close to putting Otto in the brace," he told my mom while examining the X-ray of my femur.

Perhaps back at the Cleveland Clinic he told my parents about the brace, but it was news to me. I'm guessing telling a six-year-old boy he will be in traction was traumatic enough.

They didn't want to add to the suffering by informing me about a brace. Upset and shocked, I said, "I'm going to wear a brace?" Disbelief bellowed from my belly.

"Yes," he replied in his kind manner. "I'll be right back," he said leaving the room.

Mom held me and said, "It is going to be all right, Junior. The brace is going to help you." I felt safe wrapped up next to her bosom with her telling me everything was going to be okay. News of the brace was a shocker but Mom's soothing words and physical embrace ensured me that everything, indeed, was going to be all right.

Dr. Sphere returned. He was holding something that looked like it came straight out of Dr. Frankenstein's lab. A full-metal device with a boot at the bottom and laces at the knee and upper thigh. "This is the type of brace you will be wearing. I want you to see it and also have a proper fitting because soon you will be wearing this."

Instead of feeling scared, I was filled with wonder. There was something intriguing about the brace, almost macabre. This cold metal was going to envelope my warm-blooded leg and deliver it back to normal. The brushed metal, rubber, canvas, leather, and lace apparatus encased my entire left leg from hip to heel to heal me.

"Take your shoes and pants off," the doctor said.

I untied my shoes, leaving them right there where I stood, dropped my pants and handed them to Mom.

"You must be seated when you put the brace on," he

instructed. I sat down in the chair.

"This is like putting your leg into a pair of pants, but this pant leg is sturdy, it's metal not fabric. It's not flexible. You will walk straight-legged or swing your leg around to move forward."

I slipped my foot into the thigh-wide opening at the top of the brace. Dr. Sphere guided my foot through the brace, past the knee-lock and nestling my foot securely into the brown leather lace-up ankle-high boot.

The sole of the boot was affixed with two leather straps connected to a spindle at the base of the brace. It had a sprocket aligned with it. On the outside of the sprocket there was a hex nut to which an Allen wrench would fit to adjust tension on the foot and leg. Just as I had been in traction to separate the femur, the brace provided a tautness, creating reverse traction to drive the ball of my femur back into the socket of my pelvis. The very bottom of the brace was a flat rectangle piece of metal, which is what touched the ground when I walked, not the boot. The metal was thick, sturdy, and small, about the size of a business card. There was a protective black rubberized pad surrounding it. It was like a brake pedal and that's exactly what it was intended to do: protect me from slips and falls and grip the ground beneath me.

Dr. Sphere laced and tied the boot, the knee-guard, and thigh-guard. Once secured, my leg was suspended within the device.

"Let's see how you walk with this," he said.

With Mom looking on, smiling, I began to walk around the room. It was anything but one foot in front of the other. With one foot in an orthopedic boot and the other in a cotton sock, I began to hobble as awkwardly as a newborn colt. Feeling clumsy, I tried to find my footing. It was problematic and embarrassing. The doctor sensed my pain and came to my emotional rescue. He stood on my right side and put his left arm around my shoulder. He began a very simple cadence and said, "Walk with me. Right foot down, swing the left around, right foot down, swing the left around." Mom was beaming. I'm sure she recognized progress and saw me as being on the road to recovery.

"We will get him fitted with the proper size, Mrs. Borsich. In two to three months he will be able to walk with the corrective brace."

"How long will he have to wear the brace?" Mom asked as I continued to circle about the room in just my shirt, underwear, and brace. I was ready to move on from my horizontal hell to my vertical victory.

"It will take three years before he is able to walk properly without the brace."

He could have said thirteen, thirty, or thirty-three years. It really didn't matter. All that mattered was I would begin to walk.

"Will he be fine after that?" she pressed the doc with her concern.

"Yes, perfectly fine. He can run, jump, swim, ride a bike, play sports, whatever he likes. It is absolutely critical that he always wears the brace except when bathing."

With the good news delivered, the doc helped remove the brace. I pulled my leg out of it, got dressed, put my shoes on, and bounced out the door. The traction had never gotten me down; I rolled with it right outside my bedroom window and beyond. But now, knowing the end of my traction was drawing near, enthusiasm raced through every bone in my body.

Once home and after sharing the good news it was back to bed, my mother wrapping the green foam and the ACE bandage around my leg and putting me in traction. She reassured me, kissing my forehead, "Pretty soon, Junior, you will be able to go out and play with your friends."

"I know, Mom." I really did know. It wasn't the next visit, but the one after that when I had the feeling in my bones that *today is the day. Today is the day I will walk out of that doctor's office in a brace.* I was seven years old and after being flat on my back for nearly a year in traction I was ready to kiss that fifteen-pound weight goodbye!

At Dr. Sphere's office a familiar sight was in the corner: a brace. A brand-new brace wrapped in a heavy-ply clear plastic bag. There was also an ankle boot in the bag, separate from the one that was attached to the brace. Neither the doctor nor my mom needed to tell me to get undressed. I kicked my shoes off and dropped my drawers. Mom and the doc looked at each other, nothing was said, but they knew I was anxious to have that metal wrapped around my leg. Doc pulled the brand-new brace out of the bag, and its matching shoe for my right foot. Having sat in that same chair two months ago, I was now an old pro at putting a brace on. I slid my foot through the top of the opening and guided it all the way into the boot. The doctor laced the boot, then the knee and thigh guard. "This is the boot for your right foot," he told me. Cumbersome looking, it had a five-inch solid cork heel with a rubber sole. The traction, coupled with the length of the brace, created a substantial differential between my left and right leg. The elevated right boot was necessary to compensate for the difference. Slipping my right foot into the boot, the doctor laced it and tied it into a knot. "How does that fit?" he asked as he pressed down on the tip, seeking my big toe.

"It fits fine."

"Not too tight?"

"No," I replied.

"Okay, stand up, young man."

I rose from the chair. I felt like a giant, not only physically but emotionally. The brace and platform boot not only increased my height, but I felt protected with it. Nothing was going to hurt me with this metal around my leg and massive heeled boot on my foot.

"Junior you got so tall," Mom said, teary-eyed as I stood nearly eye-to-eye with her.

"Go ahead and walk around the room," said Dr. Sphere. "Mrs. Borsich," the doctor explained, "you will need to rip the outside of his pant leg and add a zipper or put snaps on it because his pant leg will not fit over the brace. Before he puts his pants on, we need to cut a slit in his pant leg." He grabbed a pair of shears and offered them to Mom. Mom took the shears, placed the pants on the desk and began to cut away on the outer side of the left leg from the very bottom up until about the knee.

Sitting back in the chair, I drove my stiff leg into the pants. I put my right leg through the other pant leg and followed up with the boot. I was ready to hit it. I was upright and walking and I didn't care about the tear in my pant leg. It was air conditioning, because I was going mobile on that summer day. Ready to be kissed by the sun and all its glory. It was a new day!

Dad took a few pairs of my pants and modified them to fit over my brace. Using the outer seam as a guide, he directed the huge fabric shears making a slit from the hem to the knee. With a hammer and metal dowel he pounded the silver snaps in place. I used to get joy from ripping the snaps open. It seemed like a quick-change artist or a circus performer would have that type of wardrobe. Despite being hindered by a brace and a clunky cork shoe, nothing held me back.

The fall of 1967 arrived. On the first day of second grade I boarded the bus, hobbling and swinging my left leg in tightly since the steps were narrow and didn't permit a full swing with the brace. I held onto the chrome rail with my left hand and pulled myself upward.

"Good morning, Otto," Mrs. Hamilton, the bus driver, said. "It's nice to see you."

She hadn't seen me since the first grade, prior to my diagnosis. I returned her greeting and walked down the aisle, looking for a seat. Everything stopped. All eyes were on me. One gal, Nancy Meyers, made eye contact. She blurted in a televangelist manner, "You can walk!" Her comment was understandable. No one in Brownhelm knew exactly what was wrong with me. They only knew I had lain in bed and couldn't walk. But on that September day, the morning sunlight beaming through, they watched a miracle board that bus.

I adapted; I never wanted special treatment, nor expected it. I was just a kid who had something wrong with his leg. Granted, my left leg was immobilized. I couldn't bend my knee. I couldn't ride a bike, they wouldn't let me join Little League, I couldn't run as fast the other kids in my neighborhood. Yet abnormal as my life was, I felt completely normal. I still ran, although in an unorthodox manner. While I didn't play Little League, I played baseball with my friends. I climbed trees, went exploring in the woods. During recess I swung in the swing, went down the slide, hung from the monkey bars, got on the teeter-totter and did all the things a young boy growing up in the Heartland would do. I played kickball, too. I was usually the first one picked. Despite my lack of speed, once the classmates saw me wallop that ball with my cork shoe, they all wanted me on their team.

I do recall getting preferential treatment once, from none other than a Medina County Sheriff's Deputy at Chippewa Lake Park in Chippewa Lake, OH. It was a popular amusement park. The whole family was there for the annual Ford Plant Picnic. I was approached by the officer and he asked me, "Do you have Perthes disease?" Odd coming from the deputy, but to a seven-year-old boy he was a policeman—and don't all policemen know everything? "Yes," I replied. He then began to tell me he had a son with Perthes disease who was in a brace just like mine. About that time Mom appeared. "Is there's something wrong, officer?" He explained about his son.

"I'm Deputy Sheriff Reed," he said as he pulled out a small pad and pen from his left breast pocket. "Here is my name and badge number. Just show this to the person taking tickets for any ride. This will give you front-of-the-line privileges."

"Really?" Mom questioned. I am sure she was in disbelief. For me, I'd just won the lottery. Front-of-the -line privileges!

"Yes, ma'am, enjoy the day."

There were thousands upon thousands of people in the park that day. The compassion and generosity of Deputy Reed touched us both. His name and badge number were priceless. Every time Mom presented it, the entire family proceeded to the front of the line.

Summer turned into fall. With every changing season I was X-rayed to check on the progress. Dr. Sphere kept the X-rays on file and would show them to Mom to compare them to the previous ones. It was slow going, but into the second year it was evident the femur was making headway to nestle into the pelvis. Dr. Sphere told us, "It will be a year to eighteen months more."

A year to a year and a half: that meant sometime in the fourth grade I would be free. I was already calculating in my head and measured time by the seasons to figure out how many more trips it would take before I could remove the brace for good. In somewhere between four to six seasons I would be able to kiss that brace goodbye! Every night I took it off and laid it to rest right next to my bed. Every morning I woke up and there it was to greet me. While in the fourth grade I found a source of inspiration that stayed with me to this day. My brother Doug, three years my senior, taped a quote by Calvin Coolidge on the outside of his bedroom door. The quote is simply known as *Press On*. I remember reading that at around age nine. The quote reads:

> "Nothing in the world can take the place of persistence. Talent will not; nothing is more common than unsuccessful men with talent. Genius will not; unrewarded genius is almost a proverb. Education will not; the world is full of educated derelicts. Persistence and determination alone are omnipotent. The slogan 'press on' has

solved and always will solve the problems of the human race."

I asked big brother what those big words meant: persistence, determination, omnipotence? He handed me a dictionary. "Look it up." Like an injection of knowledge and wisdom from Noah Webster himself, those words flooded my bloodstream, filling a young heart with courage and inspiration. Little did I know, as a disabled child I was a living example of those words. Children can be the cruelest, especially to other children. I heard all the derogatory comments: gimp, handicap, peg-leg, hop-a-long, cripple. Those words stung but I never let the poisonous tongue of their messenger infect me. Instead, I corralled my dreams and stampeded into the great wide open with a brace, a bum leg, and a cork boot. Those insults were good for me. They tested my mettle. I pressed on.

No longer bedridden, my imagination went full throttle. My ambitions were fixated on two things. First, I was going to join the Navy and serve my country. I dreamt of faraway lands, captivated by thoughts of journey and adventure. After serving in the Navy, I was going to become a chef. I had known what I wanted to be when I grew up as far back as kindergarten. Little boys wanting to join the Navy is not so far-fetched. On the other hand, growing up in the sixties and wanting to be a chef was an unusual, if not extreme, career choice. When I was a kid, chefs were like ghosts. You knew what they were, but you never saw them. The only chefs I knew were Julia Child, who billed herself as the French Chef, Graham Kerr the Galloping Gourmet, and of course Chef Boyardee who in fact was a real chef from Italy and made quite a name for himself in Cleveland. His ubiquitous product line is still sold in supermarkets today.

It was only a matter of seasons before the brace would be removed. In the Spring of 1970 the cherry blossoms burst open on the tree in my front yard. It was the end of April and I could not have received a better birthday present. After examining the latest round of X-rays, Dr. Sphere said, "Congratulations, the femur is in place and you may now remove your brace."

Starting with the expert diagnosis at the Cleveland Clinic, and thanks to the love of my parents and siblings, and the care from my teachers, my Brownhelm buddies, Dr. Sphere and the staff at St. Josephs, I beat Perthes disease. I finally booted that brace and was no longer handicapped or having the appearance thereof. I regained full control of my left leg and to this day I can dance with the best of them. Just like Calvin Coolidge said, "Persistence and determination alone are omnipotent." I pressed on. At the tender age of ten, given what I had been through the previous four years, I discovered what it meant to Taste the Freedom. I have been tasting it ever since!

■

*"Man never made any material as resilient
as the human spirit."*

BERNARD WILLIAM

*For I know the thoughts that I think toward you,
saith the LORD, thoughts of peace, and not of evil,
to give you an expected end.*

JEREMIAH 29:11

■

APPLE SPICE CAKE

½ cup sultanas

3 cups all-purpose flour

1 teaspoon ground cinnamon

1 teaspoon ground nutmeg

1 teaspoon ground allspice

½ teaspoon ground cloves

½ teaspoon salt

1 teaspoon baking soda

1½ cups light brown sugar

4 eggs

1⅓ cups vegetable oil

1 teaspoon pure vanilla extract

3 cups half-inch diced, cored & peeled granny smith apples

1 cup chopped walnuts or pecans or a combo

Preheat oven to 350°F. Butter and flour a 10-inch Bundt pan. Cover sultanas with hot tap water to plump for 10 minutes and then drain. Sift together flour, spices, baking soda, and salt. In an electric mixer combine sugar and eggs on high speed. Slowly, in a steady stream, add the oil, then add vanilla. Blend in flour mixture on low speed until just incorporated. Do not overmix. Add apples, strained sultanas, and nuts. Pour batter into prepared pan. Bake for approximately 1 hour 15 minutes, or until a toothpick comes out clean. Cool in pan. Once cool, shake pan to loosen cake. Turn onto plate, and dust with confectioners' sugar, or drizzle with powder sugar glaze, or warm caramel sauce.

CARAMEL SAUCE

1 cup light brown sugar
1 stick unsweetened butter
¼ cup evaporated milk
1 teaspoon vanilla extract, or one whole bean split and scraped
Pinch of salt

Combine all ingredients in a pot. Cook over medium heat for about 5 to 8 minutes or until the mixture thickens. Serve with the cake.

Taste the Freedom.

CHAPTER 7

ROAD TRIP

MUSICAL PAIRING: Goes great with "Hot Fun in the Summertime"
SLY AND THE FAMILY STONE, VINTAGE, 1969

M Y BROTHERS CORNERED ME AFTER my performance. I was belting out James Brown's "Papa's Got a Brand New Bag" and "I Feel Good," and although I didn't sing any Elvis songs, I had his moves down. Gyrating the pelvis, just like Elvis. This was pre-Perthes disease, so I was getting on the good foot and doing the bad thing at five and six years old. Full-on spin, splits, strut, stagger steps and slide. Loved me some JB as a kid and still do. Seeing him on TV was fascinating and his moves kept me mesmerized.

We were at Grandma Simonelli's beach house. It was a hot summer night in Warwick, Rhode Island. I was raising the mercury a little more by holding my very own talent show in front of my aunts, uncles, and cousins. After I was done moving and grooving, I would take a bow, latch onto the brim of my white newsboy style hat and pass it around for tips. I usually made somewhere between three to five dollars. That is when my older brothers stepped in. Maybe they were embarrassed, envious, or truly as they said, shamed. They told me I had to stop singing and dancing because the Simonellis thought we were poor and that I was panhandling to get money for the family.

"Forget you!" I told them. "That's my candy money!" Money to buy Chuckles, Sugar Babies, Necco Wafers, wax lips, Charms Blow Pops, and a six-pack of wax bottles with the flavored fluorescent fluid in them—whatever that liquid was. Money to be spent at the arcade on pinball, or Skee-Ball. Money for the merry-go-round so I could try like mad to get the brass ring. Money for an ice-cream cone, or better yet, my favorite, doughboys. I continued to shake what momma gave me and passed my hat for the greenbacks.

Back to those doughboys. They're a Rhode Island thing: simply fried dough tossed in powdered sugar. While there is nothing new about fried dough, you can consume the warm tasty gut-bombs at nearly any street festival or county fair. Go to New Orleans and they are called beignets. But only in Rhode Island are they referred to as doughboys. There is a place right on the beach in Warwick, Iggy's Doughboys and Chowder House, established in 1924. Nearly a century later it still stands, serving their famous balls of fried dough. A must stop whenever I visit my second home.

For thirteen years straight, from 1956 to 1969, the Borsichs road-tripped from Ohio to Rhode Island to visit the Simonellis. I loved going up there, seeing all my relatives from Mom's side of the family. All those Simonelli siblings were thrilled to see their sister, Rosie. We would hit the road at the crack of dawn and head east for the almost 700-mile eleven-hour journey. Mom packed sandwiches, snacks and sodas. Dad drove straight through, only stopping for gas and to answer the call of nature. Of course, they both kept busy answering our constant question, "Are we there yet?"

"There" was Warwick, and the beach was known as Oakland Beach. We would arrive sometime just before sunset. Aunt Francis was usually the first one to greet us. Once we entered the house, in typical Italian style, we each got a suffocating bear hug and a kiss on the cheek followed by a loving pinch on the cheek. The first words out of her mouth weren't, "How are you doing? How was the drive here?" They were, "Are you hungry?" Whether you were hungry or not, you were getting fed. Usually some type of pasta and salad, oh, and sweets. Lord have mercy, there were always sweets. Aunt Francis was fond of saying, I don't have any money, but we have plenty to eat.

One of the mainstays in the Simonelli household when my mother grew up was *spaghetti aglio e olio.* Spaghetti with garlic and olive oil. With thirteen kids to feed, pasta, garlic, olive oil and a little red pepper flake goes a long way. Other staples were pasta fagioli and polenta, usually with tomato sauce and cheese, and if they could afford it, a meat sauce. As my mother often reminded me, she was a Depression baby, and that was Depression-era food. There was never any shortage of food in the Simonelli household. If you were hungry at the Simonellis, it was your fault. They preached *mangia* as gospel, it was the eleventh commandment. If you didn't eat, it was a sin. If you were sick, of course the only way to get better was to eat!

One year we were about an hour away from arrival. All of us boys were in the back seat. I was in the middle, Doug to my left, and Mike to my right. They were both fighting over a pillow, pulling it back and forth in a tug-of-war. As my brothers were grappling over the pillow, a freak accident happened. Doug's finger rammed into my eye and went knuckle deep. I sent out a shriek that would burst your eardrum. Fluid ran out of my left eye and I was blinded. The irony is, parents always warned their kids, *You're going to poke your eye out!* That is damn near what happened.

Dad stayed calm and drove as I continued to scream. Mom, frantic over what happened, kept an attentive eye on me. Once we hit Rhode Island, Mom's hometown navigation skills kicked in. She directed Dad to drive to her sister Mary's house, the closest home we could get to first. Once there, the family went inside as I waited in the car to be rushed to the ER.

Dad and Uncle Jake drove me to the hospital. I really wasn't in a lot of pain, but I still couldn't see, and I kept my hand over my eye in case my eyeball tried to pop out. I was scared. Despite the horror of the accident, I remember Uncle Jake yelling at somebody, "What the hell you lookin' at, banana nose?" That took my mind off my eye and made me laugh. Into the ER we went. The doctor shined a pin light in my eye and asked me how many fingers he was holding up. I couldn't tell him. It wasn't that I couldn't see at all, everything was blurry. He flushed my eye for a few minutes, then put a gauze pad over it, followed by an eyepatch.

His orders were simple: keep me in darkness for three days and don't let me eat any solid foods. I could understand the darkness, not wanting the right eye to overcompensate for the weak one. I did not understand the *no solid foods* though.

I recall Dad asking the doc, "Is he going to be all right?"

The doctor told him, "I didn't detect any tear on the eye, but he took a direct jab to the eye socket. He may or may not see out of the eye again, or if he does, his vision may be permanently blurred. The eye could heal itself, and then again, it may not. After three days, if his vision is not better, bring him back to the hospital."

So that is how I spent my first three days of vacation. With a pirate patch over my eye, I laid in the cool stone basement at Grandma's. No one called it a basement; it was referred to as a root cellar. That's where they stored all the root vegetables, the slight chill being perfect for keeping vegetables fresh. I stayed in the dark with a steady diet of broth and Jell-O.

When we arrived at Aunt Mary's, Mom called her sister,

Francis, to tell her the story of the eye accident. After a long pause, in typical *mangia* fashion, Francis said to Mom, "What the hell you doing at Mary's? She doesn't have anything to eat." Never mind the trauma to my eye and the possibility I might never see out of it again. All Aunt Francis could think of was feeding us. Three days later my eye healed itself, and I could now eat with my eyes wide open! I was fortunate nothing serious happened.

I was rushed to the ER on another occasion, along with my sister, Paula. We had second-degree burns. Not from fire, boiling oil, or scalding water, but from Mother Nature.

Minus protection to block the sun's UV rays, we spent a day of fun in the sun and surf at the Atlantic Ocean. At the end of the day, our bodies were a fire of flesh, a mass of silver dollar-sized blisters. My fair-skinned sister and I were in such stinging pain we could barely walk. Mom and Dad drove us to the ER. I remember it hurt just to put a shirt on. Inside the ER, my sister and I sat at the ends of beds in the same examination area. The heat radiating off my body was unbearable.

The doctor arrived, took one look at us and asked, "What happened?" What did he think? Someone mistook us for lobsters and tried to cook us in a pot of boiling salted water? That's certainly what it felt like. The saltwater and sun created a double whammy, not only burning us but completely sucking our bodies dry. My body felt like a blast furnace. After taking our vitals, the doctor then delivered, not one, but two shots. I don't recall what they were—I'm guessing an antibiotic and a tetanus shot. One in each shoulder. My sister got her shots first. I remember the doctor with the syringe in his hand and a needle so long that when I saw it I began to scream for my sister. He inserted the needles into her scorching flesh. I was next.

"Don't think about it, Junior," Paula said, trying to comfort me.

Don't think about it? The double dose of three-inch needles getting ready to pierce my skin? Pretty hard not to think about it. The epidermis was torched right down to the dermis.

They placed us in wheelchairs and took us to the front entrance where Dad was waiting in the car to pick us up. The nurses tried to assist us. The pain was so tortuous I wouldn't let them touch me.

Back at Grandma's house, I set my foot down to exit the car. The pain that shot up my legs when simply putting one foot in front of the other was excruciating. It felt like hot lava was pumping through my circulatory system. Dad picked me up, cradle-style, and carried me into the house and laid me on the bed. As gentle as he was, blisters popped with every step. I wailed as I watched the water ooze out of the blister. It shriveled, forming a dead skin rumple that hung from my forearms, exposing rounds of raw pink skin. Dad cracked opened the jar of burn cream and placed some on the end of a tongue depressor to apply. Even the application of that analgesic ointment was painful.

I was out of commission for two weeks. I'd learned a healthy respect for the sun and, to this day, I am hypervigilant about the big yellow ball of burning gas a million miles away. I still love the ocean, salt air and sand. However, I am not a sun worshiper and I do not go to the beach without lathering myself with SPF 45 and jamming a monster-size umbrella in the sand to create shade. My closest friends call me *Moon Tan*. I'll wear that moniker with good reason: I'm never going through that hellish pain ever again.

Packing up the car and heading back to Ohio was always bittersweet. While it's true there is no place like home, Rhode Island was, and always will be, a second home to me.

A few years into the road trips, Dad got a wild hair and decided to buy a camping trailer. That became our little home on the road. The summer vacation to the Simonellis now became a camping trip. He would unhitch the trailer and park it on the side lot next to Grandma's house. The metal scripted nametag at the rear of the trailer identified it as a *Roamin' Home*. All the Simonellis loved it. They were proud of their father's Roman roots and referred to it as a Roman home.

One year, driving back from Providence, Mom wanted to go to NYC. Mom had big ideas about going to Rockefeller Center, Radio City Music Hall, Macy's, St. Patrick's Cathedral—the full Monty—every must-see NYC attraction. Dad wasn't having it, although he compromised. There we were, smack in the middle of the greatest city in the world in the Ford LTD Country Squire Wagon with its faux wood paneling, towing the *Roamin' Home*. A real-life precursor to *National Lampoon's Vacation*. Amid a sea of people scurrying beneath skyscrapers that soared higher than silos. This concrete jungle of glass, steel, and concrete was as dense and impassable as a thousand-acre Midwest cornfield. Dad navigated through the cluster of cars in the maze of Midtown Manhattan. I don't know what Mom was thinking. Nor can I comprehend Dad going along with the idea. I am sure Rosie imposed her will on the NYC side-trip, which amounted to a massive detour on our way back to the Buckeye State.

"That's it, there it is," Dad said. My brothers and I, heads poked out the window, necks strained, looked upward. There it was: the Empire State Building, the iconic monolith made famous by the gargantuan gorilla in the silver screen classic *King Kong*.

At the time, this held the title of being the world's tallest skyscraper, peaking at 102 stories. Other than that, there would be no other sights to see. No pretzels from the street vendors, no Sabrett dogs, no pastrami on rye, or a slice of pizza pie. But what that little excursion did was tease my taste buds to bite the Big Apple. Even though I wasn't even in my teens yet, I knew New York City was for me. I don't recall if we took the bridge or the tunnel out, but I was going back in. That was one seed Rosie planted, albeit indirectly, and about fifteen years later that seed would bring fruit. Despite Mom's erratic idea, it was the genesis for me to return to Gotham.

The last time we drove to Rhode Island was the summer of 1969. That was the year Grandma Simonelli died. She passed away shortly after we returned home, July 16 to be exact. I remember when the phone rang with that news. Mom broke down; she was bawling. I'd never seen her cry like that. She was mad at herself. After receiving the call, Mom kept saying, "I knew I should have stayed there, I knew Mom didn't have much longer." Perhaps her instincts were telling her to stay. A premonition nudging her that summer would be the last time she saw her mother. Grandma was frail, in failing health when we last saw her. She stayed in bed frequently. When she did get up, she could barely walk, always needing assistance. Age and motherhood had taken its toll. She had been perpetually pregnant, giving birth to thirteen children and she'd spent many long days cooking and cleaning.

Those road trips were fun-filled and packed with priceless memories: the anticipation of seeing Grandma, a dozen aunts and uncles, and dozens more cousins every year, plus traveling to Little Rhody, as Mom called it. Then there was the ocean, the arcade, the food, the Italian-American verve so prevalent in Providence. It was a great escape from the Heartland to New England. It was a slice of American pie, giving me the taste of travel, adventure and culture at a young age. I am forever grateful.

■

Big families are like waterbed stores, they used to be everywhere, and now they're just weird.

JIM GAFFIGAN

Lo, children are an heritage of the LORD: and the fruit of the womb is his reward. As arrows are in the hand of a mighty man; so are children of the youth. Happy is the man that hath his quiver full of them: they shall not be ashamed, but they shall speak with the enemies in the gate.

PSALM 127:3-5

■

SPAGHETTI AGLIO E OLIO

1 pound dried spaghetti
⅓ cup good olive oil
8 large garlic cloves, cut into thin slivers
½ teaspoon crushed red pepper flakes
½ cup minced fresh flat leaf parsley
1 cup freshly grated Parmesan cheese, plus extra for serving
Salt and pepper to taste

Cook pasta in one gallon of salted water. Ensure it is al dente as it will cook more in the second step of the recipe. Reserve one cup of the cooking water before straining. Meanwhile, in a skillet large enough to hold the cooked pasta, over medium-low flame, warm the garlic until it becomes fragrant. Do not brown the garlic, only cook until lightly golden. Add red pepper flake and cook for about 30 seconds. Add the cup of reserved liquid to the oil. Bring to a boil and reduce by a third. Add the pasta, turn off the heat, add cheese, parsley, season with salt and pepper, toss. Let rest for about 5 minutes for the pasta to absorb the sauce and serve immediately.

Serves 4-6 people.

Taste the Freedom.

CHAPTER 8

WAR IS HELL

MUSICAL PAIRING: Goes great with "Ohio"
CROSBY, STILLS, NASH & YOUNG, VINTAGE 1970

MAY 4, 1970 REMAINS A HISTORICALLY tragic day. It was the day Allison Krause, Jeffrey Miller, Sandra Scheuer, and William Knox Schroeder, all unarmed students, were shot and killed on the campus of Kent State University (KSU). The incident is simply known as the *Kent State Massacre* or the *May 4th Massacre*.

I'll never forget my father saying, "They killed four of our own, Rosie," speaking to my mother as he read the headline from the *Lorain Journal* that chilling spring day. The Vietnam War was escalating and made shockingly real by the evening news. The jungle war attacked Main Street and advanced into America's living rooms, sharply dividing our great nation. In the process, the counter-culture was birthed. Like bayonets to the brain, the war split our national psyche. Students throughout the country protested and it came to a brutal apex at Kent State. In the aftermath, hundreds of campuses were shut down. KSU closed its classrooms for six weeks. Less than a week after the shootings, over 100,000 people marched on Washington to protest the war. The Peace & Love crowd cleverly placed carnations in the barrels of rifles clenched by National Guardsmen and began to wage a war of their own, a war of consciousness. Fighting the power with Flower Power.

Sixty-seven shots were fired in thirteen seconds, taking the lives of those innocent students who had been going about their business, not actively involved in the campus protest. William Knox Schroeder was from Lorain, my father's hometown, which drove the horrific act even closer to heart. Schroeder was an Eagle Scout and Honor Student in high school. He was gunned down in the back with a single shot from an M-1 rifle while innocently walking to class over 100 yards away.

Kent State, a mere hour drive from my idyllic lakefront hometown of Vermilion, was now thrust front and center in the national spotlight. Crosby, Stills, Nash, and Young wrote the iconic rock ballad *Ohio* from the disastrous events of that fateful day. That song was the title track to the rapid end of the Woodstock nation. David Crosby once said that Neil Young calling Nixon's name out in the lyrics was "The bravest thing I'd ever heard." Crosby noted at the time that it seemed that those who stood up to Nixon, like those at Kent State, were shot. Neil Young did not seem scared at all. The war raged on, tearing this country apart. I was sickened at the tragedy. As a tender ten-year-old, I didn't know much about war other than brave men from my hometown were going to Vietnam and some were coming home in pine boxes. Others were designated MIA. It was easy to spot who had a family member on active duty—there would be a simple blue-star banner hanging in the window of the house. When the blue star was replaced by a gold star, that meant the ultimate sacrifice: a family member had died in combat.

In just a short month after the May 4th Massacre, classes at Brownhelm Elementary School would end for summer vacation. I was in the fourth grade; Mrs. Louis Simon was the teacher. The day before summer break, Mrs. Simon informed our class that we could wear anything we liked on the last day of school. That gave me a green light to be outrageous, to be outlandish, to be Otto. I rushed off the school bus and burst into the house, "Mom! Mom! Mrs. Simon said the class can wear anything we want to school tomorrow!" My mind whirred at the speed of a hovering hummingbird. What to wear? What to wear? Flashes of ideas popped through my head like paparazzi's flashbulbs.

Go minimal: wear my bathing suit as a kick-off to summer. How about going as an astronaut to celebrate the glory of Apollo moon missions? Perhaps I'd be a cowboy. I would saddle up and ride into the fifth grade come

September. Yippee yi yay! Maybe I'd go as a hippie. My older brother, Duane, had enough tie-dye, colored glasses, beads, fringe and headbands to make Timothy Leary proud. This was Halloween without the candy. A full license to dress to impress, or better yet, frock to shock! As a lover of American history, I flipped through the pages of a Civil War book. It was the brilliant but brutal Union General William Tecumseh Sherman who blazed through the South with his scorched-earth policy and is credited with the phrase *"war is hell."* That had a radical ring to it, a ring that resonated with this whippersnapper. It was my Eureka moment. The '60s were still fresh. Amid social upheaval of the biggest counter-culture movement in American history, I was going to make a statement on the last day of school.

I gathered the tools to construct my one-of-a-kind outfit: my mother's fabric shears, a black marker, and a yellow short-sleeved sweatshirt. I cleared off the top of my dresser to use as a worktable. The large shears dwarfed my small hands as I maneuvered them to cut off the sleeves, producing a tank-top effect. This scrawny kid was going to flex his muscles after donning this masterpiece. I eagerly tossed the newly cut sleeves aside and began my Dali moment—for this was surreal. Fat, chisel-tipped ebony marker in hand, I began to draw a one-line diagram of Brownhelm Elementary School. It was a simple two-story brick building, a large boxy structure that was easy enough to replicate on the garment. Taking my time and exacting as much detail as possible, I completed the drawing. The black lines against the bright yellow made for a strong contrast and a perfect canvas for the elementary art. The two-toned color scheme was symbolic as a yellowjacket, the predatory wasp set to unleash its stinger on its unsuspecting prey. I drew a large plane flying above Brownhelm School, dropping bombs directly over it. On the back of the shirt were the bombs bursting in air. Brownhelm was blowing up! The *piece de resistance* was Sherman's immortal words scrawled in broad, black, bold letters on the backside of the wide elastic band at the base of the sweatshirt. Those three bold-faced words were my John Hancock. Little did I know this unique garment would become part of a classic tale. This is my favorite childhood story. Indeed, a radical but profound expression from the eyes of a child during the age of innocence.

I showed Mom the shirt. She coolly said, "That's nice." She didn't display any anger or emotion in terms of me wearing the shirt to school. It was good enough for her. After all, Mom grew up during WW II and had seven brothers, some of whom had served. My dad was on the front lines in the Korean War. My brother, John, was on active duty during this time. Mom knew a little something about war. Although I came of age in the seventies, I bore the spirit of the sixties. The '60s were the most tumultuous decade in our nation's timeline: a decade of mayhem, civil rights, race riots and assassinations, and the greatest counter-culture movement in America. The defiance of that decade defined my DNA. I was a radical kid who questioned authority and certainly marched to my own drummer. With the repercussions of Kent State still reverberating throughout the nation, especially in Ohio, Brownhelm Elementary School was about to be rocked on a sunny early June morning.

I walked off the bus, entered the school, and walked up the well-worn concrete steps to the western side of the building. I swaggered into the classroom with confidence and went to my desk. As I sat down, the pandemonium hit the fan! A human lightning bolt struck and electrocuted the room, zapping everyone inside. My classmates were shocked. "Ohhh! Otto's got a curse word on his shirt! Otto's gonna get a spanking!" Hands over mouths, and fingers pointing, they were stunned to see a swear word on a classmate's clothing. I basked in their attention. *That's right,* I thought, *check me out: I am not making a statement, I am the statement.*

Mrs. Simon walked in the room. It was the last day of school: three months off from teaching. I'm sure she was happy. Her happiness turned to surprise and amazement when she found the entire class out of control. I sat calmly, centered in the eye of the hurricane as the classroom spun out of control because of the profanity on my shirt. They were all pointing and screaming, "Mrs. Simon! Otto's got a curse word on his shirt!"

"Class! Take your seats. Be quiet!" Mrs. Simon ordered. She took quick strides to my desk. There she stood, green eyes glaring at me through cats-eye frames. Her face burned red as I stared right back. "Young man, stand up!" A silence enveloped the classroom. Maintaining eye contact with her, I slowly rose out of the rickety desk chair and stood casually, if not boldly, before her. She gave me the elevator look, scanning me from head to toe and back again. She paused at my abdomen, seemingly searching for something: for that, that *curse* word that had churned her classroom into chaos. Her anger grew visibly after seeing the front of my shirt. She then walked behind me. Faster than you can say "napalm" I felt a hand grip me. Like a puma pouncing on its prey, she took her left hand and dug her digits deeply in the nape of my neck. With her left hand firmly planted, she then proceeded to spank me in rapid fashion. Like an Uzi *rat-a-tat-tat-tat-tat-tat* firing off machine gun rounds at my rear end. It didn't hurt, and I was laughing on the inside, defiant. I'd pissed off the authority and created havoc. She must have nailed me twelve to fifteen times.

At age ten, I didn't know what *mise en place* meant. In French it means *to put in place*. However, it is the battle cry and the body armor of all cooks. Their translation can simply be distilled to one word: preparation. You must be prepared to execute 300 dinners on a Saturday while you work the grill, or any station. All your steaks, seafood, chops, pasta, minced garlic, salt and pepper, stock, sauces, pans, cutting board(s), olive oil, herbs, tomato concasse, white wine, tasting spoons, side towels, sani-bucket, and of course butter. Oodles of that sweet treat that warrants a call from the nutrition police. Everything you need to bang out 300 plates of food. When you're *en plas* you get in the zone and you rock it. If you are not *meezed,* you will be zoned out and get rocked by hungry patrons. You'll be desperate in a desperate situation as the order machine keeps spitting out tickets relentlessly.

Are you "meezed" or "*en plas*" is chef-speak to the brigade before service. "How's your meeze?" "Mind your meeze." Or, "Are you *en plas*?" In other words, "Are you ready?"

But back to fourth grade. I had anticipated a possible paddling and wanted a buffer between my booty and the board. I snagged yesterday's sports' section from the *Journal.* I folded the newspaper in conventional fashion, horizontally across the mid-section, then in thirds lengthwise. I placed the newspaper inside the rear of a pair of tighty-whiteys. For good measure, I put on one more pair of undies to secure the daily news. Guess you could call me the original smart ass, or at least a clever one.

Finished with her spanking, she fumed, "Go to the office!" She escorted me out of the classroom straight to the office. "I am calling your mother! What is your number?"

I gave it to her.

She placed her finger in the rotary dial phone and, after completing each number dialed, kept her finger in the numerical holes and forced back the dial to accelerate the call. This was the original speed dialing. "Mrs. Borsich? This is Mrs. Simon. Are you aware of what your son wore to school today?" Mom knew full well what I'd worn, but she didn't admit that to Mrs. Simon. Let's just say that Mom and Mrs. Simon didn't always see eye-to-eye. Mom always claimed to have psychic powers and knew she would call.

"He is wearing a shirt with profanity on it and it is disturbing the class."

"Disturbing the class on the last day of school in fourth grade, Mrs. Simon?"

"Yes, and you have to come to school and bring him a different shirt to wear."

The Borsich household was about a mile away from Brownhelm. It was no big deal to bring me a new shirt. But Mom never took well to authority. There was no way on God's green earth she was going to take orders from Mrs. Simon, let alone bring me a new shirt. Mom was never at a loss for words and she told Mrs. Simon, "If Otto's shirt is bothering you that much, have him turn it inside out. Goodbye." Mom shut that conversation down real quick and provided a simple, clever solution to silence Mrs. Simon.

I spent the remainder of the day with my shirt inside out, not feeling vilified but victorious because at ten years old I'd made a statement about an unpopular war and a fifty-year-old adult didn't know how to handle it. I never told Mom that Mrs. Simon spanked me. If I had, there is no doubt in my mind she would have gone to school and delivered a tirade so brutal it would have butchered Gordon Ramsey into a puddle of saline. Who knows, Mom may have even thrown in a haymaker just for the swell of it. That's how she was. She could discipline and strike her kids, but heaven help anyone else who laid a finger on them. Mom even went so far as to contact Mr. Knight, the principal. She wrote a letter demanding that Mrs. Simon was not to teach Michael, my younger brother, during his grade-school years.

Ironically, Mrs. Lois Frye, the other fourth-grade teacher, was at Kent State in the spring of 1970, finishing her degree. She was told to evacuate the campus because the school knew trouble was brewing. Campus authorities conducted a door-to-door dorm search and confiscated rocks and a rock hammer that Mrs. Frye had for a geology class. Can you imagine a fifty-six-year-old woman with a rock hammer at an anti-war student demonstration in 1970? The FBI actually came to Brownhelm to question her about the rocks. Was she going to use them to overthrow the government? Seriously?

She was incensed at James A. Rhodes, then-Governor of Ohio, who had given the order to send the National Guard to KSU. On May 3, the day before the massacre, Rhodes said of the campus protesters, "They're worse than the Brownshirts, and the Communist element, and also the Night Riders, and the vigilantes. They're the worst type of people that we harbor in America. I think we're up against the strongest, most well-trained, militant, revolutionary group that has ever assembled in America." These revolutionaries were pot-smoking peaceniks and his incendiary remarks became a flashpoint the next day when four students lay murdered on the grounds of KSU on a sunny May day. It was Governor Rhodes who had given the order to crush the Vietnam War demonstration. It was he who'd ordered the National Guard to open fire on innocent civilians, killing students who were seeking an education. It is he who is dead and buried with the blood on his hands of four dead in Ohio.

Mrs. Frye did complete her degree: magna cum laude, no less. Everyone loved Mrs. Frye. I never had her as a teacher, but my siblings did. She had grandchildren who were my age. She approached me in the hall on that last day of school. She rested her hand on my left shoulder and said, "That's right Otto, war is hell. Never forget that."

I never did. Nor did I ever forget Mrs. Frye. She impacted countless lives and ascended to the other dimension on April 25, 2009, at the grand age of ninety-five years young. The following year, in February of 2010 the site of the massacre was listed in the National Register of Historic Places.

I asked Roni Frye, one of Mrs. Frye's daughters, if her mom had any favorite recipes she would like to share. Roni told me, "Mom was pretty proud of her mashed potatoes." When I asked for the recipe Roni said, "Mom didn't have a recipe, she just made them, but they were darn good." Interestingly enough, I am pretty proud of my mashed potatoes, too. Downright persnickety, I might add. This is my mash, dedicated to Mrs. Frye, from the Brownhelm boy born to be a chef.

■

You're not a baby boomer if you don't have a visceral recollection of a Kennedy and a King assassination, a Beatles breakup, a U.S. defeat in Vietnam, and a Watergate.

P.J. O'ROURKE

Blessed are the pure in heart: for they shall see God.
Blessed are the peacemakers:
for they shall be called the children of God.

MATTHEW 5: 8-9

■

CHEF OTTO'S MASHED POTATOES

4 pounds Yukon gold potatoes, peeled, cut in quarters
1 bay leaf
Kosher salt and freshly ground white pepper, or a smidgen of cayenne
1 cup heavy cream
4 tablespoons unsalted butter

Put the potatoes in a large pot, add the bay leaf, 2 tablespoons of salt, and cover with cold water. Bring to a boil over medium-high heat, then reduce to a medium simmer and cook until the potatoes are tender. Don't boil, but simmer the potatoes. Drain, remove the bay leaf, and allow all the steam to escape to dry the potatoes. Meanwhile, heat the cream and butter in a small pan. Put the potatoes through a ricer or food mill and place in a bowl. This is a very important step to make a smooth mash. Add the hot cream and season with salt and pepper or cayenne. Mix together, taste, adjust seasoning. Garnish with fresh chives, rough chopped Italian parsley, and/or smoked paprika.

Serves 6–8.

Taste the Freedom.

CHAPTER 9

RUFUS ONE, RUFUS TWO, CHICO TOO

MUSICAL PAIRING: Goes great with "Man of the Hour"
NORAH JONES, VINTAGE 2009

D EW-DAMP PAWPRINTS SPOTTED my shirt from playing with Rufus while waiting for the bus to come and take me to kindergarten. I loved that cuddly little furball mutt, with his long, black curly hair covering his eyes. I always wondered how he saw with his canine curls covering his peepers like an English sheepdog. I think he had some French Poodle in him and Lord knows what else. Rufus was small, maybe ten pounds but he looked much bigger with all that hair. He, of course, was the family dog, but to me, he was *my* dog. Depending on the season, we would romp around in the grass, jump in the leaves, or traipse through the snow before the school bus arrived. He was always the last to see me before I left for school, and the first one to greet me when I came home. Like any dog with keen senses, he was perceptive beyond definition and loyal as lapping waves to a shore. His unconditional love was beyond reproach. If the human race was capable of absolute love like their four-legged friends, there would be no need for Jesus Christ to return. Their love, like God's, is perfect, faithful and eternal. Isn't it remarkable that a member of the animal kingdom is the embodiment for how to love in God's kingdom?

Humans could take some lessons from dogs. Starting with being happy every day. Enjoy the great outdoors. Go ahead, stick your head out the window. Drink plenty of water. Take a nap. Be present and listen. Keep digging, you never know what you may unearth. Never bite when a gnarl will suffice. Accept every Scooby Snack with gratitude. Explore everything; sniffing doesn't hurt, either. Greet treasured friends and family like you haven't seen them in years. Never pretend to be something you're not. When a friend is having a bad day, sit still, be quiet, and comfort them. Be present and don't hold grudges. Be a best friend. Enjoy every meal as if it is your last. Protect who you love and those who love you. Practice obedience. Have dogged loyalty. When scolded, forgive, turn that frown upside down, go back and make friends. Never turn down the opportunity to go on a joyride. Be joyful about what you have. Give more than you receive. Appreciate a simple life.

There is a reason why dogs are called man's best friend. Yet there is a special bond between a boy and his dog. Rufus and I were as inseparable as epoxy. When I was away, he knew well before that side door opened from the garage into the kitchen that his buddy was home and it was playtime. He would jump up, flip around, circle my feet and do his best to climb up my leg. That's when I would pick him up and the loving would start; he was a big licker. All I saw were his white teeth and that little pink sandpaper tongue against his coal-colored hair. "Hi Rufus!" As he licked away with the speed of a kid devouring an ice cream cone on a sweltering day, I would laugh as his tongue tickled my cheeks, then set him on the floor for a belly-rub session. Rufus was my original best friend.

One day, while waiting for the bus, he began to bark. Along with the barking he became restless and began to squirm from the cradle of my arms. I set him down on the gravel driveway. As I did, he began to bark louder and repetitively. From behind me I heard a vehicle approaching. I turned around to see a cement truck rolling down the road. The ten-ton truck lumbered by with Rufus barking in full force. Once it passed us, Rufus tore after it. "Rufus, Rufus, come home Rufus," I yelled. The truck slowed for the stop sign at the intersection fifty feet away. Rufus continued to chase the massive truck. I kept screaming for him. He ran right under the truck. Brake lights glowing, the truck crawled to a stop. There was an agonizing yelp, then silence. That painful wail sank my heart. I ran toward the right side of the truck, still screaming, "Rufus, Rufus!" I saw him behind the rear tire. He laid there, lifeless, I screamed hysterically.

What I saw, no child should see. Rufus had been steamrolled by the double-axel dual-tire configuration. Nothing remained but a flattened mass of bones, brains and blood seeping onto the tarred rural road. He never knew what hit him. The driver either heard my panic-stricken scream or saw me in his extended mirrors, or both. I stood there, traumatized. Rufus, who I'd been holding a minute ago, was now embedded into the pavement, flat as a mat.

Maddened, I wailed, "You ran over my dog!" Tears erupted like a burst water balloon.

"I'm sorry," said the driver. "Where do you live?"

I just pointed. He left his truck at the intersection and we began to walk toward the house. As we approached the front door I bolted into the house, leaving the truck driver behind. Mom was in the kitchen. She looked shocked when she heard me bawling like a baby. Before she could ask what was wrong, I blurted out, "Mom, Rufus got run over." She grabbed my hand and sped toward the door where the cement truck driver stood.

"I'm sorry, ma'am. I never saw your dog," said the man.

Mom instructed me to stay right there outside the front door as she walked with the driver toward the cement truck. She turned around and came back to the house and grabbed a brown paper bag and went right back to the truck again. The driver had a large, wide shovel on the truck. I watched him scoop up my best friend and place him in the bag.

What does a mother say or do to comfort her five-year-old son who just watched his dog get pulverized by a massive cement mixer? There wasn't much she could say or do other than hug me and tell me, "It's going to be all right, Junior." She held me and did the best she could to calm me down. I felt as if that truck had run me over, too. However, I was still living, and Rufus was gone. "I should have never let him go, Mom. I set him on the ground and he took after the truck." I thought I was to blame for his death. Mom kept holding me, telling me it was going to be all right. I missed the bus that morning and Mom drove me to school.

Later that afternoon my eldest brother, John, twelve years my senior, placed the bag holding Rufus into a shoebox. Shovel in his hand, we headed deep into our acre-sized backyard. As we passed an area where old railroad ties and rocks were piled up, John paused and began to look through the rocks. He picked up a flat stone and handed it to me.

"What's this for?" I asked.

"It's for Rufus," he said as we continued on until the very end of the property line. John put the box down and speared the shovel into the sod and dug. I knew what was next. Rufus would go into that hole, never to be seen again. With John serving as excavator, undertaker, pallbearer and priest, he knelt to retrieve the cardboard coffin. On his knees he lowered Rufus into the grave. "Say goodbye to Rufus, Junior. He is in dog heaven now." John then began to return the dirt from where it came. The first couple of shovels were gentle as he eased the soil onto the top of the shoebox.

I watched John fill the hole bit by bit. Every shovel full of dirt hit my heart like another nail in a coffin. My insides bled as I bit my lower lip to tourniquet my emotions from rising to the surface.

With the last bit of dirt returned to the grave, John tamped down the soil with the back of the shovel. Laying the implement down, he picked up the tablet-shaped stone. He looked at one side, then the other. It was flat, oblong and whitish grey. He extended his right leg outward and rubbed the rock against his blue jeans, to and fro along his thigh, wiping it clean. Putting the stone on the ground, buffed side up, he pulled a Magic Marker out of his pocket. John began to write on the slab as I watched: R U F U S. He then cleared a shallow area, an inch or two deep, dead center, and placed the tombstone on top of the grave and snugged the dirt up against the stone.

I had just lost my best friend, but I wanted to be brave for Rufus, and brave in front of John, too. I certainly didn't want to cry in front of my big brother. Mom sure, but never John. I looked up to him as any boy does toward their big brother. I'd cried my eyes out in front of Mom. Consequently, my tear ducts were empty. I couldn't muster a tear if I tried. I was stunned to a state of numbness. It's one thing for a boy to lose his dog. It's entirely another to witness the ghastly manner in which he died.

Life became as empty as the half pint of milk drunk during kindergarten break. My bouncing black ball of rambunctiousness was gone. My shirts were no longer soiled with paw prints. No four-legged bundle of joy saw me off to kindergarten or welcomed me home. But I soldiered on, even as Mom, Dad, and siblings raised the subject of another dog. There was only one Rufus.

Two months after his death, I discovered my precious pooch left me the best gift ever. My neighbors, the Thomases had a bitch. She was a mutt named Rags because of all the splotches of color against her predominately black canvas. White, khaki, brown, and a patch of Irish-setter red adorned her chest. Rufus answered the call of the wild and as a member of the species who created doggie style, he got busy with Rags.

The Thomases informed us Rags had a litter and said to come get a free pup. There were a total of seven pups in the litter. Six of the puppies looked like Rags, predominately black with patches of earth tones scattered on their tiny bodies. But the seventh pup was all black with curly hair. He looked just like Rufus!

Of course, we took the pick of the litter and brought him home. I was euphoric. That pup was the spitting image of Rufus, a gift from the grave, and from above. It was a miracle. The pain that had struck my heart a couple of months earlier had been replaced with joy. I had a brand-new puppy, a male, who looked just like his father. Naturally, I named him Rufus. We kept him in the kitchen in a cardboard box with a cozy bed of thick foam padding and an old sweatshirt.

Rufus One had been in the family about two-and-a-half years before I entered the world. The difference between the two dogs was that I was able to watch this weeks-old pup grow up. I grew closer with this Rufus because of that. We did everything Rufus One and I had done together. I tried to teach him how to fetch without much success. It didn't matter. I was the happiest boy on Earth.

A year later, I was outside on a late spring morning playing with Rufus, waiting for the bus to take me to school. Mrs. Gringle was the school secretary. She lived two homes west of me. Every morning she would drive by in her white four-door Ford LTD Landau and wave on her way to school. But one day my jet-black mutt raced after her and, like his father, met an unfortunate death.

Mrs. Gringle walked to the front door and told Mom what had happened. She and Mom picked Rufus up from the roadway. I had just lost my second best friend in the world.

When John came home from school that day he grabbed a shovel and a stone and we proceeded to the rear acreage. Just as he had a year ago, John dug a hole and we laid Rufus Two to rest. I was devastated. There were no more miracles involving Rags. Rufus was dog gone, dead and buried. I went from the happiest little boy in Brownhelm to the saddest in the state of Ohio in a nanosecond.

I knew it was an accident, just like the cement truck had been an accident. But that didn't make it any easier. I never saw the cement truck driver again. Mrs. Gringle was my neighbor. I saw her drive past my house every day when school was in session. I also interacted with her as all schoolchildren did; she collected the lunch money for the week. I knew she felt horrible for weeks after Rufus was killed. She couldn't even look at me at school or when she drove by in the mornings.

We didn't own any more dogs for a few years. Then sometime in the early '70s my mother and little brother Mike and I were in Vermilion. A house had a sign posted: free puppies. We pulled into the drive, met the lady who owned the home, and she took us into the garage to see the litter. There were four puppies. She proceeded to tell us they were peek-a-poos, a Pekinese and poodle mix. They were all varying degrees of slate grey, black and white. The lady had already given them names. Harpo, Groucho, Chico, and Zeppo. She told us the puppies were so playful and made her laugh, so she decided to name them after the Marx Brothers. We decided to take Chico. He was more Pekinese than poodle with straight coarse hair, black eyes and had an overall salt-and-pepper color. Chico didn't tip the scales at more than five pounds once fully grown. Like all pups, he was full of curiosity and energy. I enjoyed playing with him, and not to compare, but he was no Rufus. Of course, I was now a pre-teen and had outgrown the romance between a boy and his dog. Mom loved him though, and that's all that really mattered.

In the summer of '77 I was working as a cook at McGarvey's Restaurant in Vermilion. Mom, Dad and Mike were away on an overnight trip to Amish country. During the summer months, we kept Chico outside on a retractable leash and brought him in the house at night. Knowing I would be gone at least eight hours, I ensured his bowls were topped off with water and food as I headed to work. I was scheduled to work two p.m. to ten p.m. that day. It was overcast, threatening to rain, and the sky had clouded over in an ominous fashion. Thunderheads were rolling in. Not long after I started my shift the word spread that rain was coming down in sheets outside. Booms of thunder and cracks of lightning detonated above us. I thought of Chico and how he must be getting soaked but figured he would be fine. It was inevitable that he'd get wet but at least he was sheltered from the canopy of the tree he'd been tied close to and could hunker down around the trunk.

The deluge continued. Some hours later, during a lull in the dinner service, I opened the back door of the kitchen. The precipitation was maddening. Rain water gushed through the parking lot like snowmelt on the Colorado River. There hadn't been rain like this since 1969 when floodwaters rose and submerged McGarvey's a good two feet underwater.

After I punched out to end my shift, I bolted to my '67 Pontiac Belvedere, hit the wipers on max, and slowly started my rain-swept four-mile drive home. Visibility was all of maybe ten feet. Once home, it was a mad dash from the car door to the front door, although it would've been impossible for me to get any more wet. I just wanted to get out of my drenched clothes, take a hot shower, watch Johnny Carson, and go to bed. Which is exactly what I did. I hit the mattress as the rain furiously pounded the two windows of my corner bedroom and bolts of lightning snapped and strobed the midnight sky to the bass of rolling thunder in the distance.

It wasn't long after my head hit the pillow that I was off to dreamland in a nice warm bed.

The morning sun awakened me. "Chico!" I jumped out of bed and threw on pants and a shirt, grabbed my sneakers and headed toward the door. I'd totally forgotten about Chico. I ran to the back yard where he was tethered. "Chico! Chico!" The songbirds were chirping, but there was no barking to be heard. "Chico, Chico!" My voice grew louder as I drew near where he had been secured to a metal auger corkscrewed into the earth. I was now running in ankle-deep water and it was growing deeper. I was thinking the worst but hoping for the best. Frantic, I yelled his name over and over, as the water reached knee level.

As I got closer to the tree I saw the black nylon leash. I grabbed the leash and tugged. I'd found Chico. The poor dog had drowned. Bound to a retractable leash, he could not outrun the rising water. He extended the leash as far as he could, trying desperately to out-maneuver the torrent.

There was an immediacy to death when Rufus One and Rufus Two died. They didn't suffer, but I certainly did after they departed. In some peculiar way, Rufus One's death adjusted me to Rufus Two's death.

All life, be it human or animal, should be able to die in a dignified manner. Unfortunately, Chico suffered a horrific death trying to flee a force of nature without being able to escape. Sadly, but befittingly, I grabbed a box, a shovel, a stone, a marker, and did what John taught me a decade earlier.

Rest in peace Rufus One, Rufus Two, and Chico, too.

You transported this old man back to boyhood for some dog-gone good memories.

■

Outside of a dog, a book is man's best friend.
Inside of a dog it's too dark to read.

GROUCHO MARX

For that which befalleth the sons of men befalleth beasts; even one thing befalleth them: as the one dieth, so dieth the other; yea, they have all one breath; so that a man hath no preeminence above a beast: for all is vanity. All go unto one place; all are of the dust, and all turn to dust again. Who knoweth the spirit of man that goeth upward, and the spirit of the beast that goeth downward to the earth?

ECCLESIASTES 3:19-21

■

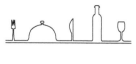

RUFUS TREATS

½ cup all-purpose flour
½ cup whole wheat flour
¼ cup wheat germ
¼ cup brewer's yeast
pinch salt
1 tablespoon smoked paprika
1½ tablespoons rendered bacon fat, melted
½ cup low-sodium canned beef stock room temperature,
plus more for glazing

Preheat oven to 400°. Whisk together flours, wheat germ, yeast, salt and paprika. Make a well and place the bacon fat in bowl with stock. Mix thoroughly until a dough forms. On a lightly floured surface, roll the dough out to ⅜-inch thick. Shape the biscuits using a dog bone-shaped cookie cutter. Alternatively, use a store-bought dog bone biscuit and cut around it with a knife to create the bone shape. Or make a cardboard dog bone stencil suitable for your dog's size. Place on a lightly greased or parchment-lined baking sheet. Bake for 10 minutes, then brush with additional stock and bake 10 more minutes. Turn the oven off. Permit the dog biscuits to dry completely in the oven for approximately 1½ to 2 hours. Remove from the oven and store in an airtight container.

Makes approximately 4 dozen.

Taste the Freedom.

CHAPTER 10

A HAMMER & A DREAM

MUSICAL PAIRING: Goes great with "Working Man Blues"
MERLE HAGGARD, VINTAGE 1969

HE THICK CARDBOARD MAILING TUBE arrived in the spring of 1960. Inside that long brown cylinder were the master plans. The map to Dad's treasure. Dad was a tinkerer. Even as a young boy, he took trips to the junkyard to find scraps to build something. In high school, he built an operational steam engine. In shop class he drew the plans and constructed a solid maple seven-drawer desk that has been passed down as a family heirloom. Dad was a regular Handy Andy who could fix or make anything.

We lived in a modest three-bedroom, one-bath home on one-and-a-quarter acres. The roof over the garage was flat, not peaked. With two-by-fours, Dad built a four-foot-high frame and nailed them into a repetitive X pattern around the perimeter of the roof. Painting them white improved the overall aesthetic of the home, adding texture and dimension to the roofline. Another enhancement was installing a sliding-glass door on the back side of the house that led into the kitchen. Before that home improvement, it was just a standard 80-inch x 36-inch wooden door with a small window to peer onto the acre-plus yard. I remember Dad removing the existing door off the hinges. Then, with a power saw and crowbar, he ripped out a five-foot section of studs, sheetrock and insulation. My young eyes were fascinated by the big job Dad was doing. The roar of the saw, the ripping of wood, the smell of metal splitting lumber as sawdust drifted around his work boots mesmerized me. In quick order, what had been a door and a wall became a sizable opening.

I watched him frame in the large rectangular opening using an old-fashioned wood level. I wouldn't be a bit surprised if the level was something he had as a kid growing up. It must have been four-foot long, taller than I was at the time. In the center and on either end were the slim glass tubes with the thin black lines to measure the bubble to ensure surfaces were level. Holding the level vertical under Dad's watchful eye to make sure the bubble was dead center became my job as he hammered in the frame.

With a boxcutter, and my older brothers there for the heavy lifting, Dad slit the cardboard container open and they removed the sliding-glass door from the box. With some drilling, screwing, hammering, and caulking, Dad and my brothers made quick work of the installation. Mom planted a big kiss of approval on Dad's lips.

Like a kid with a new toy, she was thrilled at the novelty of gliding the door back and forth.

"Hey, Rosie, I just installed it, don't wear it out," Dad joked. Watching him remove the old door, ripping down a wall, and installing that giant windowed door was nothing less than amazing in my eyes. I was elated just watching what my handy Dad could do. That huge door, like Dad, let the sunshine in, filling the kitchen with light.

Continuing his remodeling phase, he bought this heavily grained natural wood paneling and stained it antique white. He resurfaced the kitchen cabinetry and installed new knobs that he'd made on his lathe. He was doing a makeover before the term became popular and making Mom jubilant in the process with a naturally sun-drenched home.

Another kitchen project was building a large L-shaped banquette with removable seats. Beneath the seats was ample storage for canned goods and nonperishables. He upholstered the seat in white Naugahyde and finished it with decorative brass tacks. My siblings and I used to cozy up in the banquette. Nobody else in the neighborhood had a banquette. Nobody else in the neighborhood had a dad like mine, either. My dad was handy, my dad could build stuff. The family loved sitting there: it felt like a restaurant. Mom's good cooking made it feel like a restaurant, too. That same table that we dined around was the one Dad dreamed upon.

Every spring, when Mother Nature's riot of color would erupt from its winter dormancy, Dad would bloom into action. Just as those perky daffodils burst, their sunshiny petals swaying with the promise of a new season, Dad would continue to feed the seeds of a childhood dream.

Grabbing the stepstool, he would place it in front of the mahogany hutch where we kept all the good china and silver— the fancy tableware that was only used at Thanksgiving and Christmas. Perched on the top step, Dad would reach high over his head to grab the tube, the master plan for his dream. I was five, and the tube and its contents were as old as I was.

"Hey, Junior, come here. Dad's got something to show you," he'd say. He would sit down in the mahogany captain's chair and place me in his lap. Tapping the tube in a downward motion against the kitchen table, he would force the contents down to one end. Removing the end plug, he'd open the tube and pull out its contents: a large roll of heavy manila paper and an unusual three-sided ruler.

The triangle-shaped measuring device seemed odd to me. It wasn't the standard twelve-inch wooden ruler I was accustomed to in kindergarten.

"What's this, Dad?"

"That's an architect's scale, my boy."

Well of course it was . . . didn't every dad in Brownhelm have an architect's scale?

Dad would unfurl his dream. Opening the off-white rolls, he'd expose the underside: a dense blue, almost indigo sheet with white lines of varying width. They were blueprints. Dad grabbed four of the kitschy mugs Mom kept in the hutch and employed them with good use, posting one at each corner as paperweights to hold down his dream.

Dad subscribed to the *Cleveland Plain Dealer.* The first Sunday of the month featured the house of the month. One month a particular house struck his fancy. It was a colonial-style two-story. Officially it was coded Design H-50. By architects' terms it was known as a bi-level. It was also referred to as a raised ranch, high ranch, or a split ranch. He sent away for plans that came from an architect in New York City. They were priced at $35 for four sets, plus $5 shipping and handling. It seemed like a mighty fancy-looking house and appeared ginormous on the blue paper. I remember saying to him, "Dad this house is really big." He told me, "That's right. It's double the size of this house."

It was a simple enough design, but what gave Design H-50 the grandeur of a stately home was a six-foot extended portico with its imposing pillars. The home suggested a Southern-plantation style.

Dad would take that architect's scale and scratch out notes on a pad. Like a chef designing his dream restaurant, Dad was designing his dream home. Granted, the blueprints weren't made to his specifications. But like any great chef, he took what he had and adapted things to his liking. Design H-50 was merely a generic recipe he was altering for his own taste.

I'd sit in his lap. He'd hold the three-sided ruler in one hand, the pencil in the other, and a chilled Carling Black Label within arm's reach. I'd ask, "What are you doing, Dad?" The answer was always the same: "I'm making some adjustments."

That's how it was, every spring from 1965 onward. He would get that stepstool, reach for those plans, unroll them, dream, and make adjustments. In 1966, my sister Paula graduated from Firelands High School. The following year my brother, John, graduated and shipped out for the navy. It wasn't much longer before brother Duane moved out on his own. The tumultuous decade of the sixties had come and gone. It was now 1970 and Dad was still dreaming, still making adjustments. By then, I was ten. I got to thinking, *how many adjustments do you need to make?* I never said anything, I didn't have to. Mom did all the talking.

Paula got married in 1971 and moved out to start her new life with her husband, Bob. With the three older children gone, there really wasn't a need for a big house anymore. It was just the five of us: Mom, Dad, Doug, Mike, and me. But Dad had the location, a prime corner lot just up the street. He'd purchased the land years before he bought the blueprints. He had picked Brownhelm as the spot for his dream home. It was a three-and-a-half-acre parcel, complete with a brook.

As a youngster I would go down there and romp around with my neighborhood buddies. We would spend hours catching frogs and crawfish. In the winter it would freeze over and we would slide on it. It was cool to hang out underneath the bridge that was built sometime in the 1800s.

Mom began to needle Dad. "Otto, you're full of #>!%. You are never going to build that house. You're a dreamer." Dad never said a word. He would simply reach for his Black Label, his dream on the table in front of him. She had the dreamer part right.

In 1973, John was stationed in Naples, Italy. He had been in the service for seven years and was on his way towards making a career of it. He surprised my folks and bought them round-trip air ticket for two from Ohio to Italy. They were gone the entire month of July. While there, they did the full tour: Vatican City, Rome, Venice, Tuscany, Capri. They even climbed Mt. Vesuvius, the only active volcano on mainland Europe. Dad, still dreaming when they hit the peak, picked up a palm-sized piece of pumice, putting it in his pocket. Who knows how old it was? Thousands of years, I'm guessing. But he had his reason for picking up that volcanic rock.

That, among other souvenirs, including cheesy mugs from various regions throughout Italy, made it back home to Brownhelm. The biggest thing my father brought back was not in his Samsonite, nor was it found in any store, marketplace, or seaside village. His soul had been stirred by the classics. After touring the birthplace of the Renaissance, soaking up the architectural splendor of the Sistine Chapel, the Coliseum, the Trevi Fountain, the Leaning Tower of Pisa and whatever else moved his creative soul, Dad brought back inspiration from the old masters of the ancient world. Intoxicated after a month-long tour of Italy, thirteen years of adjustments, and forty-plus years after being a teen with a dream, Dad called the excavator and gave the order to begin digging to lay the foundation.

In August 1973, the yellow bulldozer made its way onto the wooded lot and began to dig deep into terra firma. Dad hired a crew to lay the foundation. This gang of masons, led by a guy named Sarge, took care of business. In a single day, Sarge and his crew had the foundation built, brick by brick. My brothers and I got involved in the action too, transporting the bricks to the crew in a wheelbarrow. These guys were pros, slapping the mortar on the blocks and using their trowels like a pastry chef with a palette knife. They smoothed those edges layer upon layer, building a flawlessly smooth surface. To the north of the building were two large openings separated by a double row of bricks. I remember Doug saying to Dad, "Those are going to be some pretty big windows huh?"

"Those aren't windows, Doug-O. Those are garage doors."

That drew a big laugh, especially from Doug's little brothers.

Sarge and company hit the bricks at sunrise and packed up their pickups at sunset. The grey block infrastructure glowed white in the setting sun. The smell of freshly dug dirt and cement lingered. It was day one of Dad finally unearthing his dream. The next day, my brothers and I were assigned the task of collecting all the rocks that had been brought to the surface. The rocks were all well-rounded, with good reason. Just two-and-a-half miles straight north of the lot was Lake Erie. Over 10,000 years ago, the Great Lakes were formed when receding ice deposits slashed canyons into the land and filled them with meltwater. Thousands of years ago, the site Dad was building on was the shore of Lake Erie. The rocks had been polished round by the constant lapping of waves throughout the centuries. We found a substantial amount of flat rocks as well, which Dad instructed us to keep in a separate pile. He had a plan for those rocks.

Dad worked at Ford seven days a week. He was home by 4:45 p.m. every day. After a quick dinner he would tell us three boys, "Saddle up." That meant we were headed to the new house. Saddle up we did. Slowly but surely the house began to take shape. Working a few hours a day until sunset, and even less in the winter, Dad began to hammer away at his dream. Dad accumulated four weeks of vacation annually from Ford. That vacation time was used to build the house. Dad and his family construction crew framed, ran electric, plumbing, sheet-rocked, and shingled the way to a brand-new home.

I recall installing the sliding-glass door in the rec room. It brought back memories of watching him install the one years ago. However, this time I was an active participant, not just an observer. The glass was so pristine, so crystal clear, it was as if you weren't looking through glass at all, but a window of air. Even Dad commented, "Sucker's clean, ain't it?" Once the door was hung, Dad exited the sliding glass door to continue to work on the balcony steps. Mike and I were inside, as were the rocks we had collected over a year ago. We began to pile them in a corner not far from the sliding door.

We both noticed Dad returning. He didn't realize the door was closed. We watched him walk dead into the glass door. A thud echoed, and his face print smudged the glass. Knees buckling, arms flailing, he stumbled backward. It was as if he'd just gotten walloped by an intergalactic force-field. He managed to regain his balance. Stunned, he looked at us. Mike and I cracked up. We bolted out the door to see if he was okay, trying to squelch our laugher, which was impossible. I said to Dad, "Sucker's clean, ain't it?" Dad smiled with that blue glint in his eye, and replied, "Yeah, it sure is." He was fine, he took it on the chin, literally, made us laugh, and he laughed it off too.

The blueprints had called for a brick fireplace, but that was one of Dad's adjustments. Those well-rounded Lake Erie shoreline rocks were put to good use. Instead of the standard reddish-brown bricks, this was to be a stone fireplace, putting what came out of the earth back into the house. That pumice he casually picked up while ascending the peak of

Europe's most dangerous volcano? Dad knew exactly what he was doing. He brought that hardened lava home to nestle it in a spot amidst the Great Lakes' rocks. Clever guy my dad, always thinking. Talk about putting an ultimate thumbprint on your creation. Whenever I had company, I would always show them the fireplace and ask, "Do you see this rock right here?" I would then tell the story about my parents climbing Mt. Vesuvius.

A couple of other adjustments Dad made were quite slick too. He had an intercom system throughout the house. The command center was, of course, the kitchen. On the wall was a built-in AM/FM radio, along with all the buttons and a transmitter for the various rooms. That radio came in handy during the winter when we tuned in for school closings. It was also the source of my rock & roll when I was cooking. Dad was a huge fan of Paul Harvey, and got me hooked, too.

Now for the rest of the story. Dad obtained a large amount of cherrywood from a friend for pennies on the pound. His buddy had a substantial cherry tree in his yard and during a storm it was damaged. Dad took the tree to a mill and had the wood fabricated to his specifications. He used the handsome-grained reddish-brown lumber to make the banister in the stairwell foyer. He spun the spindles himself on his Shopsmith Mark V, an amazing all-in-one machine. It featured a wood lathe, drill press, table saw, sander, and router.

Dad wasn't a member of the *Greatest Generation,* officially defined by Tom Brokaw as those brave men and women who sacrificed and served during WWII. However, Dad was certainly one of the greatest of his generation. With the mind of an engineer, the hands of an old-world artisan, the skillset of nearly a dozen industrial and construction trades, and the heart of an artist, Dad could fix or make anything. Whether the area of expertise involved plumbing, electrical, mechanical, welding, carpentry, auto repair, radio and TV repair, HVAC, or painting, Dad had an all-encompassing knowledge of how things worked. More importantly, he knew how to fix them. I remember him telling me, "The more you know, the less you have to pay." When you were raised in the Great Depression and then later in life had six mouths to feed, you watched every nickel. It wasn't so much that he was frugal, he just wasn't a spendthrift. He was prudent, resourceful, and clever.

He even made the chisels used to shear the wood on the lathe. Sure, he could have bought them, but they were expensive. Dad purchased some heavy-duty files from the local hardware store. He ground them down to a razor-sharp angle with convex tips. The files were a fraction of the cost of the chisels offered at Sears & Roebuck.

Dad sanded the cherry ultra-fine. Then he routed a half-inch wide strip from the entire length of the railing. With a light coat of cherry stain, followed by copious coats of varnish, the stairwell had a rich handsome sheen. In that half-inch gap, he inlaid a beautiful multi-hued strip of marquetry. It was an intricate graphic pattern with a zigzag border and repetitive diamonds in succession down the center. That touch transformed the entryway into a grand foyer. Given the split-level design, there was a sizeable wall that sprouted from the lower floor up to the ceiling of the second floor. It had to be a good sixteen-foot high by ten-foot wide. It was a large blank white wall, too big and out of reach to hang art or family photos. Dad decided to cover the wall with a mural. There was no Lowes or Home Depot back then. Dad searched various stores with large selections of wallpaper. He found a mural at Sears. A considerable print, it was called Tara, and for good reason. Tara was the name of the plantation in *Gone with the Wind*. While it wasn't an exact rendering of the famous mansion from the Golden Age of Hollywood, it depicted a two-story plantation on a hill with a double-decker front porch and six classic pillars supporting the overhanging roof above the lower porch. The mural even included a long, pitched driveway lined with giant willows that led up to the mansion.

Dad put his thumbprint all over that house. Mom was thrilled and for the first time in her life, at age fifty, she owned a washer and dryer. No more schlepping to the laundromat. As the theme song to *The Jeffersons* goes, we were moving on up.

Mom loved the ocean and was crazy about swimming. She wanted a built-in pool. Dad delivered on that, too. Not just any pool would do. Dad oversaw the construction of an octagonal swimming pool that their grandchildren enjoyed for years. While my parents were far from rich, we lived richly in our new home. How befitting that we moved in during the summer of 1976, America's bicentennial. It was certainly a crowning achievement for my father with his keen Yankee ingenuity. For a quick minute my mind raced, thinking that Jimmy Carter would pay us a visit. It was an election year and Carter, to differentiate himself from the rest of the Democratic pack, chose to stay overnight at people's homes instead of hotels.

I thought, *Why not our home?* We had all the factors going for us. My Dad was a Merchant Marine and a Korean War veteran; he worked at Ford; was a dues-paying member of UAW 425, and had just became the proud owner of his American dream.

Was it wishful thinking, or just my imagination running away with me? Or was it Camelot's kiss that surfaced from the subconscious, summoning me to be connected with yet another future president? After all, we were now living in our own White House. Wouldn't that be the coolest? Well, the peanut farmer from Plains never arrived.

Moving into our home during America's 200th birthday, the love of my motherland soared. Dad, a first-generation American, born from parents who left Budapest for a better life, had carved out a life of his own. How appropriate the street where he built his dream house was named Sunnyside Road, and how fitting for this chef to grow up on the aptly named road as well.

Dad had built a house worthy of royalty. The king was finally in his castle. Along the way, I learned valuable lessons. My father was the embodiment of *Press On,* reflecting the words once said by Calvin Coolidge: "The slogan 'Press On!' has solved and always will solve the problems of the human race."

Don't listen to naysayers, always do your best, and have a dream. Dreams generate vitality for the spirit. They give us a reason to awake every morning and move one step closer to bringing our dreams to fruition. They breathe life into the depths of our soul. What is your dream? Have you inched closer to it today? The only thing standing in the way of your dream is you. It's a discipline, choosing between what you want right now and what you want most. Dad taught me to be different. Not for the sake of being different, but for the invaluable trait of being authentic. Stay true to yourself.

Dad had a hammer and a dream. He planned, persisted, and made adjustments. After thirty years, he nailed it. That dream home still stands today on the northeast corner of Sunnyside Road. It is, and always will be, a testament to the tenacity of my hero, Otto George Borsich Sr., a helluva man.

Keep hammering. It's hard work to build a dream.

■

Every spirit builds itself a house;
and beyond its house, a world;
and beyond its world a heaven.
Know then, that the world exists for you:
build, therefore, your own world.

RALPH WALDO EMERSON

Therefore whosoever heareth these sayings of
mine, and doeth them, I will liken him unto a
wise man, which built his house upon a rock: And
the rain descended, and the floods came, and the
winds blew, and beat upon that house; and it fell
not: for it was founded upon a rock. And every
one that heareth these sayings of mine, and doeth
them not, shall be likened unto a foolish man,
which built his house upon the sand: And the
rain descended, and the floods came, and the
winds blew, and beat upon that house; and it
fell: and great was the fall of it.

MATTHEW 7:24-27

■

THERE ARE FEW THINGS DAD loved more than chicken paprikash. It reminded him of that special place: home. My mother was an amazing cook. Of course, she learned from her mother all the great classic Italian dishes. When she married my father, she became versed in Hungarian cuisine. Mom grew up with the mentality that if your husband was not happy, the wife was not doing her job. This recipe is in honor of my Hungarian roots. It was a staple in the Borsich household. When I want to prepare something unique, or even cook for a potluck dinner, this is my choice. I can make it in my sleep. It constantly brings raves and sweet memories. It steers my soul and drives me home. It's a genuine connection to my Budapest blood. Food is magical that way: it transports you to another place, another time. While goulash is the national dish of Hungary, chicken paprikash is Hungarian soul food at its finest! *Jó étvágyat! (Bon appetit).*

CHICKEN PAPRIKASH

Four strips of bacon cut into one-inch pieces
One whole chicken cut in quarters
Salt and pepper
One large onion, julienned
One green bell pepper, julienned
3 cloves of garlic, minced
3 tablespoons of paprika, or more (you can never have too much paprika)

2 cups of chicken stock
½ cup of sour cream
1 tablespoon of all-purpose flour or cornstarch

In a pot, cook the bacon until crispy and remove, keeping the rendered fat in the pot. Liberally season the chicken with salt, pepper, and paprika. Sear the chicken in the rendered fat until nicely browned, then remove from the pot. Add the onion and bell pepper, and caramelize. Add the garlic, and cook briefly over medium heat until fragrant, about a minute. Return the bacon, chicken, and any accumulated juices to the pan. Add the chicken stock. Bring to a boil, then reduce to a slow simmer. Cover and let the simmer continue for about 1 hour. You are looking for fall-off-the-bone tender. If you would like a more robust flavor, substitute smoked paprika.

As the chicken cooks, whisk the flour or cornstarch into the sour cream until fully incorporated and there are no lumps. Once the chicken is cooked, temper the sour cream by transferring some of the hot cooking liquid into the sour cream, stirring after each addition. The purpose of this is to slowly raise the temperature of the sour cream until it is very warm. Otherwise, the cold sour cream, poured directly into the hot liquid, will separate. Once the sour cream is tempered, pour it all into the pot and stir to combine. Do not let it boil once you've added the sour cream. The Paprikash is done when the sauce has thickened.

I like to sex it up a bit and use one each red, yellow, green, and orange bell pepper instead of just the green pepper. It really brings a vibrancy of color to the dish.

This may be served over egg noodles, dumplings or spaetzli *(recipe on next page)*.

Serves 4.

SPAETZLI

More commonly known as dumplings

1 cup flour

¼ cup milk

3 eggs

1 teaspoon salt

Pinch of white pepper

Pinch of turmeric optional (provides a nice yellow color)

Mix all dry ingredients, beat eggs very well, then add milk to the eggs. Mix thoroughly. Place the batter in the spaetzli maker, if you have one, and proceed to drop the batter into a large pot of boiling salted water. If you don't have a spaetzli maker, simply use a teaspoon and, holding the batter over the pot of water, drop the batter by the spoonful into the water. Technically these are now dumplings, not spaetzli. Do this in batches and cook the spaetzli until they float to the surface. Remove and set aside to keep warm. Repeat until the batter is gone. If you like, heat a large skillet with a little bit of whole sweet butter until it begins to lightly brown. Toss the dumplings in the skillet to brown them, and add a bit of chopped parsley or chives. The spaetzli will be a pale yellow.

I like to toss in a smidgen of turmeric when making the batter. The flavor is negligible, but it adds a boost of color. A shot of dry mustard gives a little kick and some fresh minced chives or parsley are good additions for the batter, too.

Serves 4.

Taste the Freedom.

CHAPTER 11

THE BOSS, THE BUZZARD, & ROCK & ROLL

MUSICAL PAIRING: Goes great with "Cleveland Rocks"
IAN HUNTER, VINTAGE 1979

This chapter is dedicated to every heartbroken Browns, Cavs, and Indians fan, the Dawg Pound, the Tribe, and the Cavs need you more than ever. Keep the faith Believeland, you are the heart of rock & roll.

WAS A SOON-TO-BE TEENAGER with a rebellious streak that ran with the ferocity and veracity of Big Daddy Don Garlits. At that time the sounds of Zeppelin, The Stones,

Hendrix, Lou Reed, Steely Dan, and Pink Floyd occupied my cassette deck. I preferred cassettes to albums—they were portable. As a child, and even today, I am rarely without some music playing in the background. I practically played the entire Springsteen discography while writing this chapter. Thanks again Bruce, you continue to inspire.

When I wasn't listening to my own choice of music, I tuned into a station out of Cleveland, WMMS 101FM. Especially during the summer. I spent many a hot day on the shore of the North Coast of America, on Lake Erie and its fun islands—North Bass, Middle Bass, South Bass, Rattlesnake Island, Sugar Island, and the biggest of all the little islands, Kelly's Island. These islands have been dubbed the Midwestern Keys, and I have wonderful memories there. On the beach, fishing, water skiing, and carousing during my teenage rage, I was always tuned into WMMS during those lazy hazy days, swinging to Heartland rock & roll.

When hunger hit on the beach my meal of choice, like all North Eastern Buckeyes, was perch. Be it a sandwich or dinner with slaw and fries, perch was just what the doctor ordered. This is the finest fish I have tasted. Perhaps it's my youthful desire for a simpler time or the sweet taste of the mild fish with the deep-fried crunchy cornmeal coating that harkens me back home.

As a youngster, nothing was more fun than casting with my Zebco 77 into that Great Lake. At times, I'd instantaneously get a nibble. I'd whip that rod back to set the hook faster than you can say "fish sticks," reeling furiously until that mustard-colored delicacy would break the surface of the water and become airborne before coming ashore. *Gotcha!* I eagerly removed the hook and placed the perch in a netted bag I had anchored to the shore with a piece of driftwood. The fish would remain in that bag, submerged, until they reached their ultimate resting place, my belly.

Perch's mildly sweet meat tantalizes the taste buds, and is one of the best-kept secrets in Northern Ohio. I have only found one place to get it: from the source. Whenever I head back to Ohio, I indulge gluttonously on the thin-skinned yellow-finned fish, and often take at least ten pounds home to share with friends. It's that damn good, and that's no fish story.

WMMS was simply known as *The Buzzard* to locals. Just like the famed sparrows of San Juan Capistrano, every year in Hinckley, Ohio, on March fifteen, the buzzards returned from their winter respite.

Cleveland has long been the brunt of many late-night talk show hosts and comedians. In a sarcastic twist by the Rust Belt City, WMMS adopted the buzzard as its mascot and has reached epic status since dominating the airwaves of Cleveland skyline some forty years ago. On what was known then as an underground radio station, WMMS 101FM was introducing The Boss. The station was responsible for the extended airplay of David Bowie, Mott the Hoople, Roxy Music, and Ian Hunter among others. The Buzzard embraced Glam Rock well before the coastal trendsetters of NY and LA. Justly so, Cleveland is the home and rightful owner of

Rock & Roll. The term was coined by Alan Freed. He was born in the Keystone State, but made his mark in the Buckeye State. Freed wanted to be a band leader, but an ear infection silenced those dreams. He played trombone in a high school band called the Sultans of Swing. Freed enrolled at Ohio State and became interested in radio. He joined the Army and was a DJ on Armed Forces radio. After the military, he landed DJ jobs at small stations in Youngstown and Akron. Locally, his popularity shot up the charts for spinning pop and jazz recordings. Freed loved the rhythm and the tune of this new style of music. He made his mark because he played the original versions of soul music, of R&B, not the faux soulless white-man cover versions.

Freed was a DJ, and the first rock & roll concert promoter. Before rock & roll there was Rhythm & Blues, often referred to as race music. It was July 1951 when Freed began broadcasting on Cleveland station WJW. With the on-air name of *Moondog*, Freed pried open a shackled door, liberating black music to be played in a white world. He would slam his fist on a telephone book and shout over the air waves, "We're rockin' and rollin' now!" Upon the suggestion of Leo Mintz, owner of Record Rendezvous in Cleveland, one of the largest record stores at that time, Freed played the so-called Negro music for white teenagers. This idea simply came from the increasing numbers of white teenagers who were buying black music at Record Rendezvous.

Boldly, Freed was the first white DJ in the nation to play black music. He was the reverse Rosa Parks of radio.

Freed had a different on-air persona than the inconspicuous, subdued DJs of the day. Freed was an excitable boy who took his listeners from Cleveland to Harlem to the Delta to the Bayou via the airwaves to sanctify their adulation for black music. He spoke directly to the swinging teenagers who displayed an unseen level of hipness in the Ozzie & Harriet era. Freed began to promote concerts featuring the music he played on the airwaves. On March 21, 1952, he was the genius in organizing a five-act show billed as the Moondog Coronation Ball at the Cleveland Arena. It was the first rock & roll concert ever organized. Crowds overwhelmingly surpassed the arena's capacity. The authorities shut down the concert due to overcrowding and a riot nearly erupted in the process. The Cleveland Arena capacity was 10,000 people however, due to counterfeiting, nearly 20,000 young rockers tried to pack a space designed to hold half that amount. The concert was also live broadcast over WJW, certainly another first, in radio and rock & roll.

The concert poster stated, *The Most Terrible Ball of Them All* and *Featuring These Sensational Stars*. The lineup included Paul Williams' Hucklebuckers, Tiny Grimes' Rockin' Highlanders, The Dominoes, Danny Cobb and Varetta Dillard. The ticket price was a whopping $1.50 in advance, and $1.75 at the door. Paul "Hucklebuck" Williams was a blues and R&B saxophonist. Hucklebuck was one of the first saxophonists to apply the honking sound affiliated with the tenor sax which became the trademark of rock & roll and R&B throughout the '50s into the early '60s. Williams is best known for his 1949 hit, "The Hucklebuck," which reached #1 on *Billboard's* R&B chart. The song was a basic twelve-bar blues riff that created a dance craze of the same name.

Despite the early closing of the concert, Freed gained immeasurable notoriety. The next day, in boldface print, the *Cleveland Plain Dealer* blazed, "Moondog Ball is Halted as 6,000 Crash Arena Gate." In response, Freed explained, "If anyone . . . had told us that some twenty or twenty-five thousand people would try to get into a *dance,* I suppose you would have been just like me. You would have laughed and said they were crazy." His popularity skyrocketed and WJW increased his airtime. Freed was bringing sweet soul music to the pony-tailed, bobby-socks and flat-top varsity-jacket generation. He crumbled the vanilla-wafer world, injecting soul into wanderlust white teens. Cleveland, the nation, and world have not been the same since. It is safe to say that Alan Freed played a sweet spot in civil rights, utilizing music as a tool for tolerance.

Within that single moment in time, the Moondog Coronation Ball put Cleveland on the map in the music world. The industrial blue-collar town became the launching pad for the music biz. Cleveland introduced new acts that became nationally recognized. Freed's popularity made the pop music business world stand at attention. Soon, tapes of Freed's program were broadcast in the Big Apple. After three years in Cleveland, with the growing success of WJW, Freed moved to New York City in 1954 where he was a DJ on WINS

1010. He was paid an unprecedented sum of $75,000! WINS became a rock-around-the-clock radio station. As he spun wax in New York City, *Life* magazine acknowledged Freed as the man who started the craze we still call rock & roll.

Today, the Moondog Ball is alive and well, pumping blood through the heart of rock & roll from the North Coast of America and beyond. The Buzzard continues to soar and spread its wings proudly. The Moondog Ball, more dignified than the near-disastrous inaugural in 1952, is a controlled concert. But the spirit of the 1950s R&B and the honking horn of Hucklebuck lives on as many of the attendees dress in full '50s regalia. Break out the poodle skirts, saddle shoes, pomade, and leather jackets. Pump up your pompadour. Stash those cigs in your T-shirt shoulder. Grab your girl and do the twirl, let's rock & roll you Moondoggers! Besides the namesake for an annual concert, Moondog is the mascot of the Cleveland Cavaliers and the name of a seasonally brewed ale created by the Great Lakes Brewing Company in Cleveland.

Freed became quite a celebrity organizing rock concerts in New York City and Boston. He quickly rose in popularity, playing himself in a speedy succession of rock & roll movies, *Don't Knock the Rock,* and *Rock around the Clock* among others. *Don't Knock the Rock* exposed Little Richard to a mass audience. These movies proved to be quite popular as the youngsters could watch their music idols come to life on the silver screen much like decades later when video killed the radio star and the MTV generation was born. With a string of movies to his credit, Freed became successful in Europe.

In 1956, he cemented his status in the European Community by taping a weekly half-hour segment aired over Radio Luxembourg with a show titled *Jamboree*. Rock & roll was becoming America's biggest import, and the exporter-in-chief was Alan Freed. *Jamboree* was broadcast throughout Europe and the British Isles by a significant AM signal of Radio Luxembourg, and was simultaneously transmitted via short wave. The Beatles are on record stating their influence came from African American artists such as Chuck Berry and Little Richard, both of whom were promoted on Radio Freed. So, it wasn't just coining the term rock & roll and promoting concerts, it is safe to say Moondog directly influenced the Beatles, bringing black music via the Big Apple across the pond to lily-white Liverpool.

In 1957, Freed was host to *The Big Beat,* a weekly prime-time TV series. This was the precursor to *American Bandstand*. Ratings for the first three shows were strong, however the show was abruptly canceled after the fourth episode. Frankie Lymon of Frankie Lymon and the Teenagers was seen dancing with a Caucasian lady from the studio audience. That was taboo. This momentously offended the good ol' boys, the prejudiced management of affiliate stations in the South. Despite its popularity and growing ratings, *Big Beat* was canceled quicker than you can say "Underground Railroad." Despite the cancelation of *Big Beat* Freed went to WNEW-TV where he hosted a local version of *Big Beat* until the latter part of 1959 when he was terminated for refusing to sign a document acknowledging he received money to play music by certain artists while on the air. This was known as the *payola* scandal which erupted in 1960. It also didn't help matters much when in Boston in 1958, he point-blank told the youthful crowd, "The police don't want you to have fun." Freed was arrested on the spot and charged with inciting a riot.

Freed sank faster than an aging teen idol when he was indicted in a payola scheme. On top of that he had serious ethics and integrity issues. A conflict of interest arose when he was given partial writing credit for the Chuck Berry hit, "Maybelline." He placed "Maybelline" in heavy rotation throughout his timeslot, which in turn lined his pocket with royalties.

He was blackballed in New York City and fled to the left coast. The negative publicity did him in. Despite giving birth to rock & roll, he signed his death warrant with the payola scandal. The last years of his life weren't kind to the man. He jumped from job to job with the irregularity of a skipping 45 and moved to more cities than the concerts he promoted. In March 1964 Freed faced tax evasion indictment by a federal grand jury. Uncle Sam claimed Freed owed $37,920 in back taxes. He was broke, broken hearted, unemployed and unemployable. The man who brought rock & roll to the masses was now in debt to the IRS. Before he could answer the charges, he checked into a hospital for treatment of cirrhosis. Like most rock stars, Freed loved to party and the devil juice was the pitchfork to his liver. Alan Freed passed away January 20, 1965 in a Palm Springs hospital. A penniless, broken soul, he was forty-three years old. He always created a ruckus wherever he went and remained one step ahead of the law. He was cremated and interred at Ferncliff Cemetery in Hartsdale, New York. His ashes were later moved to Cleveland in March 2002 where they rest peacefully among the music memorabilia at the Rock & Roll Hall of Fame. David Freed, Alan's brother, has said, "He always said he wanted to live fast, die young and leave a good-looking corpse." He continued about his big brother, saying, "According to his autopsy, he died from massive internal bleeding brought on by advanced cirrhosis." The younger brother then began to wax poetic and romanticizes his brother's passing. Preferring to put a starry-eyed spin on things, he added, "He died of complications of life. Alan Freed died of a broken heart, because they took his microphone away."

I feel your pain, brother Freed. The day my knives are taken away from me, is the day I die.

Freed deeply loved rock & roll and proudly said, "I have never played a record I didn't like, nor did I forget where the music came from." As instrumental as he was in the genesis of rock & roll, he was a flawed and troubled soul. He claimed songwriting credits that weren't his, paid performers' chickenfeed on the tours he promoted, and was well-established with shady characters. Long before Bill Graham, Belkin Productions, Farm Aid, Live Aid, Live Nation, Woodstock, Lollapalooza, Bonnaroo, Monsters of Rock, and Jazz Fest, there was the Moondog Coronation

Ball. On a chilly March night in 1952 at the Cleveland Arena, the first rock & roll concert was officially born. Its proud papa: Alan James Freed. It was less than two bucks a ticket but was the genesis that would become a multi-billion-dollar global industry. Freed was among the inaugural nonperformance inductees into the Rock & Roll Hall of Fame in 1986. He was in rollicking company as Chuck Berry, The Everly Brothers, James Brown, Ray Charles, Sam Cooke, Fats Domino, Buddy Holly, Jerry Lee Lewis, Elvis Presley, and Little Richard were in the initial induction. At the inaugural dinner, Freed served the sweetest dessert. In the evening's program given to all attendees, Freed's spirit spoke the all-important last words, actually written by him decades earlier on an oldies' album as follows: "I hope you'll take my hand as we stroll together down our musical Memory Lane. 'The Big Beat in American Music' was here a hundred years ago—it will be here a thousand years after we are all gone. SO—LET'S ROCK & ROLL!"

"Rock & roll is really swing with a modern name. It began on the levees and plantations, took in folk songs, and features blues and rhythm. It's the rhythm that gets to the kids—they're starved of music they can dance to, after all those years of crooners." — ALAN FREED, NME, FEBRUARY 1956

Much like the founder of rock & roll, WMMS 101FM aka Buzzard Radio had its fair share of controversy, too. WMMS translated to Metro Media Stereo, reflecting the original owners, Metro Media. However, it has been long established among the stoner set it translates to Weed Makes Me Smile.

With a respectable 34,000 watts of power, Buzzard Radio has entertained the masses and at one time was one of the most influential rock stations in the nation. It is also the FM flagship for the Cleveland Browns. Born in April 1974 and throughout the '70s and '80s WMMS maintained a constant set of personalities that remained unchanged for years, a rarity in radio. These personalities were the brothers, the crazy uncle, the trusted rock advisor, to all those who tuned in. Their on-air persona(s) ruled radio. Like a rock & roll blitzkrieg, the Buzzard dominated the airwaves. If you lived in Northeastern Ohio in the '70s and '80s no weekend began without listening to Murray Saul, aka the Get Down Man, as he trashed the boss, that slave-drivin' SOB who owned us during the work week. Come Friday, it was the weekend and time to get down! His get-down rant was always sandwiched between The Boss, "Born to Run" and "Friday on my Mind" by Earthquake.

Consistently commandeering the local markets Buzzard Radio continually posted record-high ratings never seen before or since by other stations.

WMMS was central to introducing several known acts, including David Bowie, Rush, The Boss. Especially DJ Kid Leo (Lawrence James Travagliante) who has grown to legendary status in the broadcast world. He was with WMMS from the get-go and occupied the passenger seat during the afternoon drive shift. Devotees of vintage WMMS hail Kid Leo as the heart and soul of the Buzzard. He was responsible for breaking in such new acts as Cyndi Lauper, John

Mellencamp, the Pretenders, and scores of others. While at WMMS he was instrumental in a campaign to bring the Rock & Roll Hall of Fame to its rightful home, Cleveland.

One evening of magic occurred with the ongoing early support of The Boss by Kid Leo. WMMS not only sponsored but broadcasted live a Springsteen concert from the Agora Ballroom. This concert was independent of his national tour and was relentlessly bootlegged as The Boss and the E Street Band rocked the town that gave birth to rock & roll. This concert forged a relationship in the consciousness of Cleveland between Kid Leo and The Boss. The Buzzard was cool, as were its DJs—they were the soul of Cleveland. WMMS mastered broadcasting live concerts that were sponsored and produced by the station itself. They hosted a weekly musical interview format called *The Coffee Break Concert*. Initially, it was done in the studio where named acts would be interviewed and play live broadcasting to the heartland.

This format became so popular it moved to the Agora Ballroom. Peter Frampton, Lou Reed, Warren Zevon, and others too numerous to mention, performed on the program. *The Coffee Break Concert* series was insanely successful and continued into the '90s. *The World Series of Rock* was another feather in the Buzzard's cap. It took place at the old Cleveland Municipal Stadium. These were all-day concert affairs featuring the biggest bands of the era. Nearly 90,000 fans would swarm the old rickety stadium. With no reserved seating, the concert was strictly general admission. Radio

Free Buzzard flew high over Cleveland, entertaining its listenership with great on-air personalities, rock & roll, and an overall comforting vibe. No matter how bad your day was, you could always turn to the Buzzard to make you feel just a little bit better in that Rust Belt City.

Despite the larger-than-life existence of the Buzzard, which was awarded best radio station by *Rolling Stone* nine years in a row, from 1979 to 1987, by the late '80s WMMS format changed drastically. From album-oriented rock, AOR began searching for what was next on the musical horizon. They began to play pop, or what is known as CHR, contemporary hit radio. The Buzzard had lost his soul to an expansion of Madonna, Michael Jackson and Prince. Under OmniAmerica ownership, the Buzzard changed formats again, choosing the modern rock or alternative genre, *Nirvana, Pearl Jam, Nine Inch Nails,* etc.

There was controversy on the lakefront. Shamefully, the station admitted to stuffing the best radio station ballot box and this behavior had gone on for years. In 1988 the *Plain Dealer* broke the story and exposed the cheating. A few years later the *Howard Stern Show* came to town and broadcast via affiliate and cross-Cleveland rival, WNCX. Buzzard radio had committed an act so wicked they are lucky to still be broadcasting. This federal offense damn near clipped the Buzzard's wings. Management and staff pleaded guilty to disrupting a national broadcast of the *Howard Stern Show.*

Stern arrived in Cleveland in 1992. At that time WNCX had an Arbitron rating of thirteen. In two years, Stern went from a baker's dozen to number one. Keeping his promise, as he did with similar events in New York, Los Angeles, and Philly, when Stern reached number one in a particular city he threw a party for his fans. That is exactly what happened on the streets of Cleveland, creating a funeral for the Buzzard and the on-air personalities of WMMS that was broadcast nationwide. Every day is debauchery with Howard Stern. That's why he is the rock & roll outlaw; that's why he is How-Weird Stern. On June 10, 1994, it was a notorious day for the *Howard Stern Show*. However, it wasn't his antics that caused a furor, it was those of WMMS engineer, William Alford. Alford, wire cutters in hand, snipped the broadcast connection used to communicate to the satellite feed that delivered Stern's semantics throughout the nation. Stern soldiered on, broadcasting his program over a telephone line as engineers put together a makeshift cable as a Band-Aid. Alfred was apprehended, arrested, and sent to the slammer for ten days and fined a grand. Buzzard management claimed Alford was the sole criminal, acting alone, however a promotions director at WMMS, Heidi Klosterman, eventually pled guilty to a felony charge of attempted disruption of a public service. Greg Smith, a Klosterman colleague, also pleaded guilty to breaking and entering.

WMMS still exists, but the Buzzard is now extinct as the mascot of that once-proud progressive station that was the lifeblood of Clevelanders. I'm grateful for the rock & roll extravaganza that was Buzzard Radio and for the discovery and support of new bands. My favorite of which is Bruce

Springsteen and the E Street Band.

I grew up with The Boss. Figuratively, as the Jersey Shore is some 500 miles away from the North Shore of Ohio, but rock & roll knows no distance. He didn't like being called The Boss. He hated it, actually. He despised working for the man. He detested the conventional lifestyle of punching the clock, for he was an unconventional guitar-slinging dreamer. The members of the E Street Band called him The Boss endearingly because he was the one who delivered the greenbacks to his band while playing in small clubs from town to town. Well before earning the iconic status of America's Street Poet Laureate, he was always The Boss.

When I heard his first album, *Greetings from Asbury Park*, I, like the masses, said this guy sounds like Dylan. When Springsteen heard that comparison he changed gears, for he didn't want to be compared to anyone, didn't want to be the next *anybody*. He was determined to be the next somebody, but that album had me addicted.

I couldn't get enough. I was twelve years old when that album debuted. I'd never heard such lyrics, and his music resonated with my young outlandish spirit. Sure, I had my classic rock staples, but this Springsteen guy, he sang to me and me alone. Unlike Page & Plant who were ascending into heaven as Mick & Keith were escorting the devil. The Boss was decidedly different, rambling on like an amped-up beat poet clad in black leather, backed by a band that would rival any group of studio musicians. He was becoming a new voice for disenfranchised youth. Somewhere in the swamps of Jersey was an emerging worldly gift. He composed lyrics, defying all orthodoxy in the singer-songwriter solar system, winning hearts and minds with every misspent youth of the day.

He wrote with a swagger and bravado all his own. He burst onto the scene as a bona fide street poet. His searing lyrics bubbled like boiling road tar. Stanzas spinning like a tilt-a-whirl left me breathless as I picked up the needle on my turntable to start this fun-filled carnival ride all over again. He seemed a modern-day Shakespeare, romancing the Jersey Shore, talking of troubled teens, rebellion, hot rods and discovery of some place better than this. He wrote with the prose of Robert Frost, the adventures of Hemingway and the punch of Hunter S Thompson. When the young Bruce and the E Street Band was road-tripping from city to city, after the nightly gig the band would do what bands do. Except Bruce. He retired to his hotel room, six-string, notepad, pen and thesaurus at the ready. He has proven to be a prolific writer. With eighteen studio albums, he also graced the cover of *Time* and *Newsweek* simultaneously the week of October 23, 1975. Whereupon his father said, "Better you than the president."

His first two albums, *Greetings* and *The Wild, the Innocent & the E Street Shuffle* were critically acclaimed, but disappointing commercially. He signed a three-record deal with Columbia Records. It was make-or-break time for The Boss. He was twenty-five. He was gonna crash and burn, or he would soar. Bruce and the boys spent fourteen months in the studio developing the sound for *Born to Run*. The title track alone took six months. Bruce was possessed, maniacal in his quest to write the greatest rock album ever, a cinematographic tour de force that would set the world on fire, and he did it. In 1975, *Born to Run* was released.

Born to Run is a rock & roll juggernaut laced with intricate guitars, thunderous drums, a deep bass line, wonderous keyboards and trademark sax. It is an indomitable wall of sound, inviting the listener on a journey, invigorating them with hope and dreams. It is masterfully epic. Intertwined within the street symphony are stories of small-town Jerseyites, two-bit hustlers, hot rods, street romance—it's *West Side Story* meets *Jersey Shore,* packed with so much power and glory it leaves the listener breathless, exhilarated as they feel themselves characterized within the songs. It is difficult at best to transport a listener into a song, but The Boss did it with flair and intimacy like no other. *Born to Run* is one of the finest albums ever recorded. Certainly, the influences of Bob Dylan, Bo Diddley, Roy Orbison, and Phil Spector are there. However, the album is all Bruce. He was hellbent to orchestrate the best rock & roll album ever. Is it? Who is to say? No doubt it is one of the top albums of all time and four decades later The Boss has no signs of slowing down.

I've seen The Boss countless times. The first time was December 1979. I was home for the holidays on leave from the Navy. I received an unexpected phone call.

"Hello?"

"Ott?"

"Yeah, this is Ott."

"It's Stoner."

"Stoner, what's up man?"

Stoner was Godfrey Stonengton, a high-school classmate. He didn't do drugs, he didn't need 'em, he was inherently stoned. Stoner got the nickname as an abbreviated version of his last name but also because of his persona. He always seemed to be in some sort of haze. He stood about 5'8", skinnier than a sheath of wheat. His brown matted hair was never combed and greasier than the eggs and pork sausage served at the local truck stop. He wore glasses, thick as apothecary jars. The lenses were greasy too, as if he had used them for a napkin after devouring his truck-stop breakfast.

"I heard you were home. I know what a big Springsteen fan you are. You turned me onto The Boss. You know he's coming to the Coliseum?"

"Yeah, on the thirty-first and the first. Both shows are sold out, but I'm trying to get tickets."

"Ott, it's your lucky day, Merry Christmas. I got an extra ticket, seventh-row seat."

It was the final two days of the long-running *Darkness on the Edge of Town* tour. According to Springsteen historians the Darkness period was The Boss at his best. The epic tour launched from Buffalo on May 23, 1978 and came to an exhaustive halt on New Year's Day 1979 at the Richfield Coliseum near Cleveland. In between the buffalo wings and the heart of rock & roll was a tour that performed 115 dates!

Big cities, small cities, and college towns were rocked by The Boss and the E Street Band. He opened with "Badlands," and it was a marathon performance from there. To witness such classics as "Rosalita," "Hard to be a Saint in the City," "Growing Up," and the anthem, "Born to Run," in that era was monumental. This was the break-out Boss. Not only a lyrical genius and accomplished musician, he was an entertainer. A showman extraordinaire. He knew how to capture and captivate every member of the audience as if he or she were the only one in attendance. That was the dedication The Boss showed, night after night.

He began telling the story of when he was a child back in Freehold, NJ. With a tinkle of the keyboard and a twinkle in his eye he continued.

"When I was growing up there were two things that were unpopular in my house. One was me, and the other was my guitar. My father would always refer to that guitar, it was never a Fender guitar or a Gibson guitar. It was always that 'goddamned guitar.' But anyway, my father always said you know you should be a lawyer, lawyers own the world. And my mother she would say, no no, no, he should be an author he should write books that's a good life you can get a little something for yourself. Well, like, what they didn't understand was I wanted everything. So, my mom and dad. One of them wanted me to be a lawyer, and the other one wanted me to be an author. Well tonight you all are just gonna have to settle for Rock & Roll!"

The band erupted and the fury of the greatest live band

in the land was unleashed with the wrath of Fat Man and Little Boy. Clarence's sax screams, Mighty Max hammers his drums, Gary thumps his bass, Bruce catches air, Miami Steve's Fender shrieks, Professor Roy and Danny culminate in a keyboard crescendo, exploding their megaton power. The crowd was mesmerized by this life force better known as Bruce Springsteen and the E Street Band. With sheer exuberance they detonated the crowd and magically hypnotized them with the redemptive powers of Rock & Roll.

His four-hour marathon shows are legendary. Each and every night on stage he and the E Street Band give their all-in sweat-soaked best to the point of exhaustion. Pound for pound, there is no one who does what he does. That's why he is The Boss. When I saw him at the Coliseum it was the 114th date of the tour, yet he was as fresh and charged as a blitzing linebacker. He ruled that stage; roaming it like a crazed caged animal, he touched every corner. He climbed high atop stacks of Marshall amps and leapt off them. He huddled with the big man and got into a guitar battle with Miami Steve matching him note for note, lick for lick, demonstrating their blistering guitar virtuosity. Bruce did send the audience for a scare though. Off to the right of the stage, during the encore, he was playing Gary Bonds' *Quarter to Three*. He was saturated with perspiration and appeared to be panting. Just then, he fell to the stage. The band halted and Miami, being closest to The Boss, was the first one to render aid. He signaled for the big man to come over. The other band members were quickly approaching their downed Boss.

Grave concern was evident on everyone's face. The Big Man made a waving gesture to the left side of the stage. A man came out, a paramedic carrying a stretcher with him. After a quick check by the paramedic, they placed The Boss on the stretcher. Clarence had the stretcher closest to the head of The Boss and Miami Steve held the section by his feet. Slowly they began walking across the stage, carrying him. I thought he must've passed out from sheer exhaustion. I thought if he had been performing tonight like he had for the last 113 nights, it had it taken its toll. Just as the big man was nearly out of sight on the far-left side of the stage, The Boss sprung off the stretcher and yelled, "I ain't dead yet!" Battle ax in hand, he ripped through scorching guitar riffs as the E Street Band manned their stations to thunderously wrap up the night. Ever the showman, always a storyteller The Boss gave the crowd something to go home and talk about. I'm still talking about it.

You changed my life, Bruce. I yearn to meet you. To properly thank you the best way I can, with my gift. It will be my pleasure and honor to cook for you and the E Street Band. It is the only way to properly demonstrate my infinite gratitude for supplying the soundtrack of my life. See you at the dinner table, Boss.

■

I have seen the future of rock & roll and its name is Bruce Springsteen.

JON LANDAU

Praise ye the LORD.
Praise God in his sanctuary:
praise him in the firmament of his power.
Praise him for his mighty acts:
praise him according to his excellent greatness.
Praise him with the sound of the trumpet:
praise him with the psaltery and harp.
Praise him with the timbrel and dance:
praise him with stringed instruments and organs.
Praise him upon the loud cymbals:
praise him upon the high-sounding cymbals.
Let everything that hath breath praise the LORD.
Praise ye the LORD.

PSALM 150:1–6

■

PAN-FRIED YELLOW PERCH

THIS RECIPE BRINGS ME HOME. No matter where I live, Ohio always is home in my heart. I've caught and cooked many a fish in my day, line-caught meaty tuna fresh from the waters of Nantucket Sound and striped bass, which the locals refer to as rock fish, from Virginia Beach, and grilled fresh rainbow trout over a campfire in the wilderness of Alaska. I've surf-casted for the elusive Pompano from the Florida shore. Caught king salmon in the Kenai River. Fished off the coast of Bimini for wahoo, that delightful, sublimely delicate whitefish the Hawaiians call Ono, and no wonder, as *ono* is the Hawaiian word for tasty. Yet, despite the denizens of the deep that I have devoured, my all-time favorite still remains yellow perch from Lake Erie. Flaky and slightly sweet, simply fried, with tartar sauce, slaw and fries, when you have a bite, you're in fish-eating heaven.

10 to 12 Perch Fillets[1], thawed
Salt and pepper
1 cup flour, enough to coat fillets
2 eggs, beaten

---

1   You can certainly use other fish, like cod or tilapia, but there is nothing like Great Lakes Yellow Perch.

2 cups bread crumbs[2], enough to coat fillets
Vegetable oil, enough to nearly cover fillets in skillet

Season the fish with salt and pepper, toss the fish in the flour, shake off excess. Dip in egg, then coat with bread crumbs. In a large skillet, heat a good 3 inches of oil to 350°F. It's best to use a thermometer for this. Or, if you don't have one, simply dip a breaded fillet into the fat to test the heat. It should immediately sizzle on contact. Fry in batches until golden brown, about 2 to 3 minutes a batch. Keep the cooked fillets in a warm oven until all are fried. Serve with slaw, lemon and tartar sauce. Makes a great sandwich on a toasted bun.

Serves 4.

Taste the Freedom.

---

2 Though Panko is good and may be used instead of bread crumbs, Panko is not authentic. A mixture of cornmeal and flour is good, too, but straight-up bread crumbs are traditional.

CHAPTER 12

CAP'N EDDIE, TWICE BAKES, & SAUERKRAUT BALLS

MUSICAL PAIRING: Goes great with "Keep on Churnin' (Till the Butter Comes)"
WYNONIE HARRIS, VINTAGE 1952

T WAS SOMETIME PAST MIDNIGHT, but before the neighbor's roosters would crow, serving as the crack-of-dawn alarm in my sleepy farming community. I arose quickly, awakened from a dead sleep. Stomach agitated, queasiness percolating, I bolted for the bathroom, covering my mouth. The nightlight's soft glow dimly exposed the toilet. Just steps away from the large porcelain bowl, my brain gave the order for my stomach to immediately reverse engines. I lunged forward like a sprinter in a mad dash to the finish line.

With not a split second to spare I began to hurl chunks of seafood upstream out of my blow hole with the psi of Moby Dick. Earlier that evening, I was a land shark on a feeding frenzy, devouring every morsel in sight. Fried shrimp, fried perch, fried scallops, French fries—all washed down with fountain root beer. Gluttony is one of the seven deadly sins. There I was, bowing to King Commode, regurgitating my deep-fried piggishness, paying my penance for gourmandizing those breaded creatures of the sea. The next morning, I found out the vomiting had awakened my parents. Dad had commented to Mom, "Rosie, one of the kids is sick." She'd replied intuitively, "It's Junior; he ate too much." Mothers know.

It was my first day on the job at McGarvey's. I was fifteen and working the fryer that night, eight of them to be exact, and I was in paradise. Surely the food cost that evening spiked as I devoured the hot golden-brown goodies, eating up the profits.

McGarvey's had its humble beginnings starting post WWI. The building was originally a lucrative bait-and-outfitter shop that operated seasonally. In 1925, a couple, the Helfrichs, bought the business and changed gears from fish food to a restaurant serving steaks and seafood. They specialized in frog legs. It was a popular eatery among residents and tourists during the summer.

Four years later, they expanded the weathered, largely seasonal shack to a modern building that would be open year-round. The Helfrichs owned it until their death. Their son-in-law took over the business in 1936. It was a short run when he sold it two years later to a man named Charles McGarvey. McGarvey changed the name to McGarvey's. From then on McGarvey's began to build its reputation as a go-to spot for food and ambiance as it was a lovely riverside café with good prices, great service, and fabulous views of pleasure craft navigating their way up and down the Vermilion River.

Charlie McGarvey died in 1944 and the McGarvey family decided to sell the restaurant. That's when Charles Solomon purchased the restaurant from the McGarvey family for $35,000. There was one stipulation. The name McGarvey's must remain. After only a year of ownership, Charles Solomon was offered 70K to sell the restaurant. He declined. He, his wife Regina, aka Momma, and son Eddie owned and operated McGarvey's for forty-two years. Charles wasn't much at guest relations; he stayed in the kitchen. He was not a chef, but he did cook all the meals. Eddie and Momma took care of each and every guest in the dining room. Considering the scope, influence, and popularity of McGarvey's, to call it a Mom & Pop place would be a huge understatement. Yet, that is exactly what it was. They took the quaint café, remodeled and expanded it to seat over 300 and added a sizable bar. The new McGarvey's was huge, nearly taking up every inch of real estate of the pier it was built upon. They adorned the restaurant in full-on nautical kitsch. It was Gilligan's Island meets The Love Boat. Even the waitresses wore sailor-type uniforms. When you needed to go to the head you went across the poop deck and your gender was identified on the door as buoy or gull. Someone in today's world of political correctness may be insulted by those references.

In 1986, Eddie decided to sell it all. He cashed in his fish and chips to restaurant chain Tony Roma's. It was never the same. While Tony Roma's boasts over 150 restaurants in thirty-six countries on six continents, in my opinion a corporate cookie-cutter model simply cannot deliver the homestyle hospitality and kindness the Solomon family delivered day in and day out for four-plus decades. Tony Roma's was short-lived.

In 2000 the Vermilion Port Authority purchased the property for nearly $1 million and renamed it McGarvey's Landing. The building was leveled to provide additional boat slips. A new restaurant was built: Red Clay on the River. There is an abundance of red clay in Vermilion, hence the name from ancient French *vermeillon*. Yet all the rich history and romance of France could not save Red Clay. It dissolved too, a murky deposit of silt into the river. Currently, the spot is inhabited by Quaker State & Lube, a burger and wing joint based in Sharon, PA. The interesting part is that the co-founders of Quaker State & Lube are using Cap'n Eddie's training guide for their staff. What an honor to continue the legacy that Eddie and his parents built. Their dedication to service has come full-circle.

At McGarvey's, I learned from one of the best in the business.

The restaurant was legendary, and Eddie was the foundation behind the legend, the genius behind the hustle and bustle of what was the only drive-up dockside restaurant on the Great Lakes. While that may or may not have been true, you believed it. That was Eddie's gift. His surrogate father was P. T. Barnum. Every night he was the ringmaster of the greatest restaurant on Earth, coaching, coddling and cajoling guests and employees alike. Eddie valued people deep down and was a firm believer in relationship-building.

Old-school in his approach, his personal take on the restaurant business was summed up in five words: *service is an honorable profession.* He wrote a book about it, bearing the same name. During a recent search on eBay, I found a copy. It's a slim paperback, perhaps fifty pages long. It was going for ninety dollars. Doesn't surprise me one bit. That's actually a fair price for the priceless advice he published in the early seventies. When training new servers some of his idioms were:

"When the hand goes up, the tip goes down."

"The answer is 'yes.' What's the question?"

"Don't just wait, anticipate."

Eddie's philosophy for training the wait staff was simple: when the guests are seated in your section, you are completely responsible for their happiness. From the moment they are seated, to the moment they leave, they are in your care and it's your job to give them the best experience you can. While easier said than done, that is where Eddie set the bar for all servers. When a steak was delivered to the table, the server was instructed to ask the guest to cut into it right then to see if it was to their liking. That may seem antiquated today but consider the alternative. Server drops the food off, walks away. Your medium-rare steak is well-done. Minutes go by, you grow angrier by the minute, which now seems an eternity. Wanda Waitress is nowhere to be found. That's where Eddie excelled: he pored over the most minute details. In doing so, he trained the staff to the highest standards of service. Unlike most owners, he welcomed complaints. He loved them, actually, because that gave him the chance to make things right. He built his reputation every day, with every plate, every drink, every smile. If the guest was not happy, Eddie wasn't happy.

I remember Eddie came back to the kitchen once with a filet mignon. He brought it right to my attention. It was partially cut in half and apparently not to the customer's liking. Eddie began, "Otto, this steak was ordered medium-rare. The guest would like it cooked a little more, please."

I grabbed the filet and spread the incision made from the steak knife. Examining the perfect grill marks down to the warm rosy center, it was exactly medium-rare. "Eddie, this is a perfect medium-rare."

"He would like it cooked more; please put it in the broiler, the guest is waiting."

"That guest is crazy!" I was far from becoming a chef, but I had the attitude and ego down pat. For me, that guest didn't know how to order. For Eddie, it was about giving the guest what they wanted.

"Otto, the guest is not always right, but the guest is always the guest. The guest signs your paycheck."

Ever the teacher, Eddie schooled me in a polite fashion; he was the best at that.

He was the Sultan of Service, the High Priest of Hospitality, the Duke of Dining. Simply put, he was The Man. For nearly half a century Eddie was responsible for putting Vermilion, Ohio on the map as a dining destination—no small feat, as America was in its restaurant infancy and this unsung hero was one of the founding fathers. He dedicated his life to the foodservice industry and wrote new definitions on what service and hospitality is and should be. He even had a hospitality university. No, it wasn't a brick-and-mortar building. It was Cap'n Eddie as a professor/consultant who would go to other restaurants and train other restaurateurs about the fine art of service. Eddie was so far ahead of his contemporaries. He truly lived to elevate hospitality into a fine art and ultimately created a gold standard for owners and employees in the foodservice sector.

He touched every table every night. He had a bit of Henny Youngman in him, telling jokes, some off color, some clean, depending on the guest. That was Eddie; he knew what to do, even on those balls-to-the-wall weekend summer nights with a full parking lot, a full marina, six-people deep at the bar, and a two-hour wait. Cap'n Eddie kept his ship afloat calmly, courageously, and above all else, coolly. He was grace under pressure and knew everything that was going on in that restaurant seating hundreds of people. In three years of working there, I never once saw Eddie lose his cool. He always defused situations with humor and candor, yet he ran a tight ship. In the kitchen, there was a large sheet of plywood hanging from the ceiling with big black bold letters that read: THE COST OF DOING BUSINESS. Glued to it was one each of every single plate, bowl, monkey dish, ramekin, fork, knife, spoon, creamer, sugar dispenser, glass, cup and saucer. Beneath the objects was the price of each item.

Eddie would routinely rummage through the trash to check for waste. One time he pulled a number-ten can of applesauce out of the trash and instructed the pantry worker to use a rubber spatula and scrape out the interior walls of the can. Eddie would never tell: he would always show.

Eddie was exceptionally generous, too. In 1977 he gifted his right-hand man, Marvin Hendricks, with the keys to a brand-new Cadillac Deville. Even with those new wheels, Marv still drove his daily driver: an old rattletrap black Ford pickup. The tailgate had a well-worn, large, square sticker placed dead center. The once-bright yellow sticker had faded, but the image was unmistakably clear: a coiled snake with the words *Don't Tread on Me,* from the historical flag used during the American revolution. More importantly to Marv, that flag was one of the first ones adopted by the Continental Marines. *Semper Fi* and Oorah! Marv was a hardened patriot. Battle-tested in the jungles of Southeast Asia, he was a hero.

The MSRP on that caddy was $10,020. Marv earned it. He was the behind-the-scenes utility player who did it all. He was a macho, bare-knuckled badass; a former Marine with a couple of tours of Vietnam under his belt. He was the trusted and invaluable first mate to Cap'n Eddie. There were solid half-inch inked dark green bands circling each of his wrists. On the center of the backside was a loop tattooed with a series of links representing chain that flowed midway down to his forearm. The tat magnified his rock-hard style. He was no one to toy with. He was all business and you knew it from the get-go. A sign on his office door read:

> *If you're a salesman, I don't want to hear about your wife, your ex-wife, or your future wife. Don't tell me about your son's Little League, or your daughter's cheerleading. If I want to know about the Browns, the Cavaliers, or the Indians, I'll read the sports page. Spare me the weather report; that's the weatherman's job. Give me your best product at your best price, delivered on time. If not, I'll find another purveyor.*

He was Mr. Fix-It. He knew a little about everything. Electricity, plumbing, gas, kitchen equipment, construction, HVAC, marine repair, auto repair. He certainly saved Eddie several times the cost of that Cadillac in repairs to McGarvey's.

Marv ordered all the food and beverage, any graphics such as menus or PR-related items, he took care of payroll, accounts payable, accounts receivable, and counted inventory. He unclogged toilets, fixed the dishwasher, replaced garbage disposals. As a matter of fact, he did everything but cook. His cramped office was on the second floor. It wasn't neat and orderly, as you'd imagine a Marine's office would be. Instead, his desk was strewn with invoices, samples, a desk calendar, and an adding machine. It looked like a business battlefield. One thing I loved about Marvin and Eddie was they both served: Marv in the Corps and Eddie in the Navy. I felt they had a special interest in me, too. They knew I was on a career path at a young age and they encouraged that.

McGarvey's was known as McGoo's by the regulars. The fishermen, the boaters, the bikers, the factory workers. McGarvey's was their watering hole and Eddie was their gracious and gregarious host. There was even an unofficial club called McGoo's Derelicts. Eddie had T-shirts made with his Cap'n Eddie caricature emblazed on the front and, of course, McGarvey's Restaurant, 5150 Liberty Ave, Vermilion, OH, 44089 on the back.

Eddie honored the locals for spending their hard-earned dollars on drafts and mixed drinks. He also received free advertising in the process, giving away the T-shirts to locals. Those locals were the business's bread and butter. There was a bartender named Melanie. She was a bleach bottle blonde, as sweet as a maraschino cherry, and came equipped with major-league mammilla. She sported a Coke-bottle figure and was as hot as cinnamon schnapps. Throughout the restaurant, especially among those of the male persuasion, she was simply known as Melons. Smarts were not her strong suit. If brains were boobs, she would have reduced Einstein's right and left lobe to dumb and dumber. It was no big secret why Eddie hired her. Although two bottles shy of a six-pack, she brought the boys in, fueling their unquenchable thirst. She was bursting with a bubbly persona. McGoo's Derelicts loved the top-heavy blonde bombshell. Eddie loved her too: she was a huge asset to his bottom line. In one of Melon's more genius moments, she delivered what has become one of my all-time favorite stories throughout my career.

McGarvey's was huge—at least half to three-quarters of a football field in length. There was an intercom system that ran from the bar to the kitchen. All orders were handwritten and delivered to the kitchen. The intercom was installed to expedite orders to save time walking from one end of the restaurant to the other to send the order to the cooks.

It was the dog days of August and the heat was on. The place was insufferably packed, guests were on an hours wait. I was working the broiler, sweating in front of the burning beast: it was more blast furnace than cooking equipment. My coworker Tim and I tag-teamed the dual broilers. We cooked upwards of 500 steaks nightly.

Buzz. Buzz. Buzz. I pressed down hard on the white transmission button on the intercom. "Kitchen."

"It's Melanie."

"Yes Melanie, go ahead." Pencil in hand and duplicate pad at the ready, I waited for her order.

"I have this guy at the bar and he ordered a shrimp cocktail."

With no time to waste, I begin writing, my ear to the intercom, eyes on the beef.

Melanie continued, saying, "I looked up shrimp cocktail in *Mr. Boston* and it's not in there." Mr. Boston is the unofficial handbook for all bartenders.

I looked at Tim and he looked at me. I cocked an eyebrow, thinking *did Melons just say what I think she said?*

"Repeat that please, Melanie. The guy wants a shrimp cocktail?"

"Yes, he wants a shrimp cocktail. I never made one before and I was looking for it in *Mr. Boston*."

I was too stunned to laugh. Could Melons be that obtuse? Working in the biggest seafood restaurant west of Cape Cod, she didn't know what a shrimp cocktail was? Furthermore, she thought it was a drink?

Tim and I were hysterical.

Buzz. Buzz. Buzz.

"Yes, Melanie?" I tried to stop laughing. "Melanie, it's not a cocktail, it's an appetizer."

"Wait, what . . .?"

"It's shrimp with cocktail sauce."

"How do you make the cocktail sauce?"

175

"With ketchup and horseradish."

"And what kind of alcohol?"

"Melanie, there is no alcohol in shrimp cocktail."

"That can't be—it's called a shrimp cocktail. Otto, I know you're a minor, but do you know what goes into a shrimp cocktail?"

The conversation was ramping up.

"I told you, it's shrimp with cocktail sauce."

"Yes, you told me that, but what kind of cocktail sauce?"

After repeating the two key ingredients to her, she continued to protest, "There has to be alcohol in it, it's called shrimp cocktail."

Never argue with a child, a drunk, or a lady. I had a waitress get Eddie and let him handle the alcohol-free shrimp cocktail and Melon's misunderstanding.

■

EDDIE WAS ALWAYS ONE STEP AHEAD. He preached over and over: "Be different or be dull." He asked me on many occasions, with a fatherly hand on my shoulder, "Otto, what are you going to do to be different? When you become a chef, why are people going to choose your restaurant over other ones? You gotta be different, you gotta have a niche, a hook."

I never forgot that advice, which was not only applicable to the chef world, but life. In a sea of carbon copies, how will you stand out as an original? Blessed with the unique name

Otto, which means prosperity from its Teutonic origins, I was halfway there. As an ambitious wannabe teen chef, Eddie invested in me a wealth of advice that has paid handsome dividends throughout my life's journey. Eddie loved working with the youth. Whether they were going to continue in the hospitality industry or it was just a summer job to get through school, he delivered valuable life lessons to every person who worked for him. He led by example: he was ethical, honest, and possessed integrity without question.

Two of the signature items McGarvey's was known for were twice-baked potatoes and sauerkraut balls. The sauerkraut balls were more of a bar food or snack to nibble on. They really weren't balls either. They were shaped like mini hockey pucks. The sauerkraut mixture, composed of sauerkraut, ham, pork, corned beef and seasonings, was laid on the counter. A machine pressed into the mixture, forming the balls or puck shape. They were then breaded, chilled, and fried to order.

The twice-bakes, as we called them, must have come out of Denver because they were mile high. There was a secret to their elevation.

Patsy and Trish were the prep gals. They worked the morning shift, making all the dressings, the salad bar fixings, the twice-bakes, the sauerkraut balls and whatever was necessary to make McGarvey's kitchen tick on a daily basis. They were the heart and soul of the food production. In the summer, when it came to twice-bakes, they were baking three to five cases of russets a day—that's 150-250 pounds of spuds! They would be split lengthwise while still warm and scooped out, leaving a thin jacket. The inner potato would get whipped with milk, butter, salt, white pepper and the secret ingredient, instant potato granules, which created the volume they were known for. Sometimes I would arrive at work early or be scheduled on a rare day shift. I would watch Patsy and Trish in action. They were pros who knew the drill and had it down to a science. "You always want to heat the milk and melt the butter. The potato granules react better to the hot milk and fluff up more," they told me. The wire whisk would whip along in high gear, beating the fresh potatoes into pebble-sized pieces. Patsy would then down-shift into first gear and begin to slowly pour the #10 can of dehydrated potato particles into the fresh starch. Once emptied, she'd reach for another can. After all the dried potato was absorbed, she'd shift back to high gear again. It was amazing to watch the volume nearly double in bulk as the whisk churned powerfully at maximum RPMs. Patsy and Trish were petite ladies, I'm guessing in their thirties. They both tasted the mixture and asked me to taste it. I did, and it was surprisingly good considering they'd dumped a couple of pounds of dehydrated spuds in there.

Patsy said, "You have to taste it before you pipe it. If it's too salty, or doesn't have enough salt, it's impossible to go back and fix one thousand potatoes."

I watched them muscle the eighty-quart Hobart bowl

away from the mixer. With a plastic scoop, they manhandled the dense mixture into piping bags the size of dunce caps. They didn't use a pastry tip. The opening at the narrow end was about the size of a quarter. The potato skins were lined up on sheet trays. With the skill of master pastry chefs, they piped the warm mixture into the awaiting potato shells. It was precision in motion. I marveled at the consistency of the finished product and at the rate of speed they completed the task. They literally made hundreds of twice-baked potatoes in a span of about thirty minutes. Once completed, the potatoes were brushed with clarified butter, dusted with a whisper of paprika, and baked as needed.

I have made my fair share of twice-baked potatoes since my days at McGarvey's. While I never supplemented the mixture with potato granules, I always smile and think of Patsy and Trish, and, of course, Cap'n Eddie.

■

CAP'N EDDIE SURPRISED ME ONE DAY. It was late last century, on the threshold of Y2K. I was working at the Atlantis Resort and Casino on Paradise Island in the Bahamas. One early morning the phone buzzed in my office and flashed red. It was Josephine, the culinary administrator. "Chef, there is an Eddie Solomon on the phone. He said you were expecting his call."

The call was *unexpected*. "Yes, put him through." That

was classic Eddie, to know what to say to get straight through. "Good morning." I attempted to downplay my enthusiasm and pretended to not know it was him.

"Good morning, Otto. It's Eddie Solomon."

I could no longer contain myself and let out an exuberant, "Eddie!" I was gobsmacked to hear from him, and furthermore wondered what he wanted and how he knew I was working at the Atlantis.

He said, "I saw the article in *Nation's Restaurant News* about you."

It had been twenty-two years since I'd left McGarvey's. I had not spoken to Eddie since the early eighties.

"I was happy to read the article and proud of your accomplishments. I like to think that I was a large part of your success."

"Yes, yes you are Eddie. You showed me the ropes. I learned a lot from you, not just about the restaurant business, but about life. McGarvey's was a training ground for me."

"Well, you have done very well for yourself and I'm proud of you."

We continued on for a few minutes, reminiscing. I thanked him for calling me and was touched by his gesture. His phone call made my week, as if my respect and admiration for the man couldn't get any higher. The master calls on the student and says, "Well done good and faithful servant. You have done well with what you have learned." It was the ultimate compliment.

That was the last time I spoke to him. Eddie Solomon was one of a kind. I am grateful for his lessons and blessed to have learned them at an influential time of my life. While writing this it brought to the surface just how impactful he was during my teenage years. How he encouraged me to live my dreams, to be different and stay honorable in the service of others. There was nothing more noble to Eddie. After all, he wrote the book on it. Eddie passed on March 17, 2002 at the young age of seventy-six. RIP, grand old-school restaurateur. You were a showman, yet remained humble, dedicating your life to guest satisfaction and exceeding expectations. You were living proof of a life well-lived.

■

The best way to find yourself
is to lose yourself in the service of others.

GANDHI

For even the Son of man came
not to be ministered unto, but to minister,
and to give his life a ransom for many.

MARK 10:45

■

MCGARVEY'S SAUERKRAUT BALLS

Here, courtesy of Shelley Solomon Prueter, daughter of McGarvey's owner,
Eddie Solomon, is the recipe for McGarvey's Famous Sauerkraut Balls.

½ pound pork
½ pound ham
½ pound corned beef
2 pounds sauerkraut
1 teaspoon dry mustard
1 small onion
1 pinch parsley
2 cups flour
2 cups of milk
Beaten egg
Fresh bread crumbs

Grind together meat, onion, and parsley. Brown in a skillet. Add flour, milk
and mustard. Cook for about 5 to 10 minutes. Mixture should be somewhat
fluffy. Cool, add sauerkraut, and grind again. Shape into balls or small puck
shapes. Roll in flour, then dip in egg and roll in fresh bread crumbs. Deep fry
until dark brown.

Serves 8-10.

Taste the Freedom.

CHAPTER 13

WILD HORSES AT THE CADILLAC RANCH

MUSICAL PAIRING: Goes great with "You Shook Me All Night Long"
AC/DC, VINTAGE 1980

HAVE A DEEP, LONG-LASTING LOVE AFFAIR with convertibles. There is something special, liberating, an exhilaration that engulfs you when seated in the cockpit of a ragtop, hands commanding the leather-wrapped wheel. Shifting gears as if you were Steve McQueen. Revving the RPMs to redline and beyond. Your favorite tunes blasting from the Blaupunkt, your best friend strapped in as co-pilot, reminiscing about the good ol' days, laughing down the highway of life, riding blindly into the night.

We Americans love to drive. We live for the road trip.

That spontaneous hit-the-road impromptu attitude is heightened with the top dropped.

I owe my open-air auto romance to my sister Paula. It began in 1967. I was all of seven years old. Paula worked as an operator for Lorain Telephone. She was paid $1.29 an hour. She saved every red cent to buy her first car, a Mustang. The MSRP was just south of three grand, representing her entire annual salary. Although her favorite color was orange, she would have to settle for Poppy Red, the closest color to orange Ford offered. The beloved Pony Car, as it came to be known, took car enthusiasts and America by storm in 1964. Technically speaking, there wasn't a '64 Mustang; it was referred to as a '64 ½ because it debuted on April 17, 1964, at the World's Fair in New York. The car appeared on the cover of *Time* and *Newsweek* along with Lee Iacocca, the primary designer of the stallion-themed auto. As one of the world's most recognized automobiles, over 22,000 orders were placed on the first day of availability. The inaugural year saw nearly 425,000 Mustangs sold, producing a stampede that trampled previous sales records of any single automobile ever. The Mustang was selected as the official pace car for the Indianapolis 500 that year. In 1999, the USPS issued a thirty-three-cent stamp with a 1964½ Poppy Red ragtop.

On a sweltering summer day, the pony car corralled itself onto the gravel-laden drive. I was playing ball in the front yard with the neighbor kids when all attention became focused on my sister's new convertible. We ran to greet Paula and check out the car.

All the kids were as ecstatic as if Santa had just arrived to deliver toys. In a way, he had. That sporty car was like a magic sleigh and the kids were going to get a ride in it.

But family first.

My sister called out, "Junior, get your brothers."

I was unable to bend my left knee due to my brace, but I ran as fast as I could, peg-legging it into the house, leaving my buddies behind to ogle over the shiny new Mustang. I rounded up Doug and Mike and we headed back outside. Doug shouted "shotgun!" but my sympathetic sister and my left leg won out. So, on my initial ride in the ragtop and subsequent rides thereafter, I had permanent shotgun status.

I opened the car door and brought the bucket seat forward for Doug to step into the back while Paula did the same for little brother Mike on the driver's side. Back in those days there were no safety latches that prohibited movement of the front seat. With just the slightest push or pull the front seat would come forward, allowing easy access to the back. I landed my butt on the black bucket seat and buckled up. Boy was I feeling on top of the world, sitting in the front seat with Sis. This was a very cool car.

It's easy to see why America and the world fell in love with this iconic auto. The interior was sporty, simply adorned in black leather. No power anything: hand-cranked windows, disc brakes, manual seats and steering. The steering wheel was a tri-spoke configuration, each spoke affixed with a gleaming bar of metal with three recessed circles that progressed from small to large for an added dimension of design. Those bars were the horn. Unlike today, cars of yesteryear had large, shiny strips of steel attached to the steering wheel. The more luxurious the automobile, the more pronounced the horn was. Those like me who wax nostalgically about classic cars miss that horn. That gleaming chrome horn has been altered by padding on the wheel or replaced by a mere button snuggled alongside the cruise control on some models. Seems to me we have lost art to functionality. Gimmie back that big horn!

Within the middle of the wheel was the pony: the classic Mustang silhouette with a slim, vertical tri-color bar behind it with shades of old glory—red, white, and blue. Those colors and that iconoclastic horse galloping in midair inspired the driver to want to saddle up and take an exhilarating open-air ride of freedom!

My sister never grasped the concept of a stick shift, so her Mustang was an automatic. "I only have two feet and there are three pedals," she joked. Paula placed her hand on the T-bar shifter. Her bright red nails reflected off the shiny stainless stick. She placed her thumb over the button to disengage the shifter and put the car in reverse. Eyes on the rearview mirror, Paula then gave the wheel a full left turn, backing her new pride and joy onto the hot tarred road that bubbled from blistering heat. She paused, shifted to drive, and like a thoroughbred leaping out of the gate, we were off! All eyes in the neighborhood were fixated on one thing: Paula and her three brothers in that ragtop. There I was, front and center, waving like I was a VIP in a parade. The neighbors on Cooper Foster Park Road cheered us on.

To a seven-year-old kid, this was the coolest thing in the world. Even as the Midwestern manure touched our noses, the new-car smell came through, showroom fresh. We drove past the maze of cornfields and rich farmland abundant with grapes, apples and peaches, then headed westbound, cruising along the Lake Erie shore. The sun beamed down, warming our souls as we sang along to the radio station of choice, CKLW, known as the Big 8, out of Detroit. Its Motown and Top 40 format, as well as its megawatt broadcasting, made it one of the top-rated stations in the world. While the home transmitter was in Windsor, Canada, its 50,000 watts of power could be heard all the way to Cleveland, some 200 miles and a Great Lake away.

There is sexiness within a droptop. It's an expression of individuality, of freedom, of openness that simply obliterates the confines of a conventional car. It's an invitation from machine to man to buckle up and get down. I spent many a day in that car with Sis, grooving to the Temptations, rocking out to Creedence Clearwater Revival, and savoring every bit of American Pie. Right then I knew one day I would have a convertible. I'd fallen in love with the Triumph TR6, the Spitfire, and the Mercedes Benz 450SL.

It has been fifty years since I was introduced to the open-air auto. As of this writing, I own a gunmetal-gray Miata convertible: black top and black interior. The car is just flat-out fun. There has not been a car I've enjoyed owning more than this one. It's a grown-up go-cart—and what boy doesn't love a go-cart? Yet somewhere between a Poppy Red Mustang and gunmetal-gray Miata is another car that's near and dear to me and one I will never forget.

When Grandma Simonelli passed in July of 1969, the annual Borsich family road trip to Rhode Island to visit the Simonelli clan came to an abrupt end. The biggest reason for going to Providence every summer was for my mom to see her mom.

That changed during the summer of 1975. It was also the summer of a few firsts for me. It was the first time I ever flew on a jet. My brother Doug and I purchased our own tickets with money saved from working at McGarvey's. We flew from Cleveland Hopkins Airport to T. F. Greene Airport in Providence. It was wonderful to reconnect with cousins, aunts and uncles. As a small-town country bumpkin, Providence held a great attraction. No corn fields here. It was a world away from Brownhelm and this inquisitive kid was ready to discover new things.

With Mom and Dad 700 miles away, I was ready for adventure, to dive into unknown territory. During a portion of our vacation, we stayed at my Aunt Giovanna's house in Cranston. Aunt Giovanna and my mother could have passed for twins, even though they were a few years apart. I have tons of aunts and uncles and tons more cousins. Some of those cousins are nearly twenty years older than I, and one such cousin is Carmine.

Carmine is Aunt Giovanna's eldest son. He was the supreme *Guido* playboy. Slicked-back black hair, pinky ring, Fu-Manchu moustache, silk shirt unbuttoned to his sternum, and a gold chain with the omnipresent gold horn and hand to ward off the evil eye—a big Italian superstition. In Italy these trinkets are referred to as *cornicello* and *mano cornuto*, little horn and horned hand. No self-respecting East Coast Italian-American would be caught without their Little Italy lucky charms. Carmine had more back hair than Sasquatch and could grow a beard overnight. He woke up with a five o'clock shadow. He had a Rolodex chock full of chicks and saw more ass than a roll of Charmin. While at Aunt Giovanna's, Carmine showed up to see his visiting cousins with his big-breasted blonde bimbo-of-the week, Jessica.

After all the small talk and catching up between cousins, Carmine proceeded to converse with Doug. "Jessica's cousin is in town from California, visiting. Would you like to go to the track with us?" Carmine loved the ponies and betting on them even more. My brother Doug is a pretty straight-laced guy, one of the few people I know who grew up in the '60s and '70s who never smoked pot. I had a pretty good notion he would decline the invitation. Even before Doug answered, I was thinking, *Ask me! Ask me!*

"No, I'm gonna stay with Aunt Giovanna," said Doug.

Excellent! Yah you do that, goody two shoes, I'm thinking, hoping I could go to the track to hang out with my playboy cousin.

"How about you, Otto?"

Don't have to ask me twice, I thought.

Carmine arrived with Jessica and her cousin, Kristy. I don't know how old Kristy was, but she wasn't fifteen. She was in college in California and home on summer break. After some discussion around the kitchen table I discovered Kristy was going to school to be a teacher. As we got ready to leave, Aunt Giovanna, being a mom, said, "Be careful." She knew Carmine. I'm sure the warning was meant more for me than him.

The screen door slammed. Parked in the driveway like a motor yacht moored to a pier, was a 1973 candy-apple-red Cadillac Eldorado convertible, white top, white leather interior. Sweet! A pimp ship ready to set sail. Wide white walls, spoke wheels, fender skirts. Under the hood was a 500 cc V8. This massive mobile was over eighteen feet long, just shy of seven feet wide and nearly five feet tall, with a weight of 5,131 pounds. It was over two-and-a-half tons of magnificent machinery. The sticker on this buggy in 1973 was $9,315. El Dorado is Spanish for "the golden one." This gleaming scarlet two-ton sled was all that and more. It was simply gorgeous.

I stood gawking at the red-hot car. It gleamed like a ruby as the sun glistened off the waxed cherry finish. I had not been in such a luxurious car before. The closest I had come was my parents' Chrysler Cordoba with the soft Corinthian leather. Do you remember the commercials with Ricardo Montalbán, with his sexy accent, serving as the pitchman who romanticized the Cordoba? Well, I was now him, Sir Otto, the squire with the international name, sans accent. I was thrust in the lap of luxury, not in a Cordoba, but in a Cadillac.

I sat in the back seat behind Carmine, with Kristy to my right. Carmine started the car and the rev of the engine purred powerfully. Built like a tank, but it rode on air. It was a smooth ride and provided pounds of protection too. We were wrapped in two tons of steel. Nothing short of an anti-aircraft missile could penetrate this behemoth. I was captivated by the fancy dash, the big horn, the bigger wheel, and being the biggest car on the boulevard. With my Midwestern modesty, this car felt extravagant and my cousin Carmine was rich! This ostentatious auto was the perfect vehicle for Carmine to glorify his Guido lifestyle.

I was being chauffeured to new experiences. The world as my oyster was beginning to open. Far away from the acres of agriculture in Ohio, this young buck was ready to devour its riches. The El Dorado was the golden chariot taking me on the road of discovery.

Top down, salt air swirled about the copious cabin. The experience was a far cry from the sporty black bucket seats and pungent aroma of Heartland manure. The soulful sound of Earth, Wind & Fire on the eight-track enhanced the groove as we glided through the hot August night on the way to Providence Circle, the horse track.

We pulled into the parking lot as the sun was setting. "Watch your head," Carmine warned, as he engaged the button on the power top to bring a close to the open-air ride. A quiet hum whispered as the white vinyl began to rise upward from its recessed housing. The mechanical closing of the convertible was much smoother and hip than that of Paula's Mustang, which was done manually. The top gracefully moved forward and snuggled precisely on top of the windshield trim. With the top locked in place, we were off to the races.

I had never been to a horse track before but was certainly no stranger to the beast of burden. They galloped all around the rich farmland in my hometown. But Providence Circle was a horse of a different color. There were short men in flamboyant pastels with near knee-high boots and silly short-brimmed hats. I was accustomed to corn-fed farmers in OshKosh B'gosh overalls and John Deere ball caps.

Carmine placed some bets. I was ignorant about betting. Carmine attempted to explain win, place, show, trifecta, etc., but I just wasn't interested. I asked Carmine, "Do you ever win?" I thought it was a crapshoot, with fifteen horses running around, to try to pick a winner.

"How do you think I bought my Caddy?" he replied. "When I win, I win big."

"Really?" I wondered. Carmine knew some people; we sat

in a skybox, another first for me. There was food and drink in the private glassed room. I was in a private skybox, with a birds-eye view, food, comfy chairs . . . *oh yeah, I belong here,* I thought. We all settled down in the front row. Carmine to my left, next to Jessica, and Kristy on my right.

Despite the cool factor of the VIP treatment, I was bored with the races and started to focus my attention on Kristy. We began holding hands and then she said, "Let's get a drink." We got up and went to the back where the bar was. "What do you drink?" She began to make herself a screwdriver. I'd never been asked what I like to drink and didn't want to appear uncool. She poured the OJ over the vodka as I quickly scanned the bar. She dipped her index finger in the drink. With a wink and a whirl, she promptly put her finger in her mouth and licked it as if licking cake batter from a mixing bowl.

"Seven and Seven," I told her, after spotting a bottle of Seagram 7.

Kristy looked around. "There's no 7Up, how about Seven Ginger Ale?"

"Sure," I said, hoping I sounded cooler than I felt. Although only fifteen, it wasn't the first time I'd had a drink. But it was the first time I had a bona fide cocktail in the company of an older woman.

We took our drinks back to the seats to watch the races, but quickly realized we were more interested in each other. After a period of ogling I felt a tap on my left shoulder. I turned my gaze away from Kristy and looked at Carmine.

"Here's my keys. We'll see ya after the races are over." Carmine was eager to contribute to the delinquency of his cousin. "Don't spill anything on the seats," Carmine warned.

"I won't. I'll finish my drink here."

Carmine grinned. Kristy giggled.

I took one last gulp of the cocktail, hurling it back like a drunkard's last drink. I grabbed Kristy's hand and we left the skybox, taking the elevator down to the parking lot in search of the red sled. There it sat, gleaming in the dim lights of the track as the announcer's voice cracked the still summer night via the loudspeaker.

I walked Kristy to the passenger side, unlocked and opened the door, just as I'd watched my father do 10,000 times for my mother. Once she was inside, I shut the heavy door, walked to the driver's side and settled myself into the spacious front seat. "How 'bout some music?"

"Sure," she replied. "I like that Earth Wind & Fire."

In short order, the eight-track was amped up and the unmistakable sweet soul sound set the mood. Faster than you could say "shining star," Kristy put a lip lock on me while advancing to straddle my lap. As the pulsing beat and piercing horns summoned quadraphonic sound sensuality, Kristy became the conductor looking to make music.

Sure, I'd innocently played spin the bottle before and kissed a few girls, but this was new territory. Kristy came up for air, leaned back, placed her hands on either side of my head, and ran her fingers through my thick mane. She began unbuttoning my shirt purposefully, one button at a time.

"Ever been with a woman before?"

"Sure, I've kissed before."

"I'm not talking about kissing; I'm talking about going all the way. Have you ever done it before?"

My shirt was now completely unbuttoned, and her hands were massaging my barely hairy chest.

"Um, done it? You mean like putting it in?"

"Yes, I mean putting it in. You haven't, have you?" she confirmed.

"Nnnn, nnn, no I never have," I stammered. I had no sooner answered than Kristy began to kiss me again. I never knew "no" could make a girl so happy. She was now in a full-on embrace, her hands grabbing my hair, tugging at it, assertively massaging my scalp. Her hands fondled my ears, felt my face, bit my lower lip. Her tongue darted in and out of my mouth. She began to frantically kiss me in short bursts all over my face and proceeded to lick my ears and neck, then chest. I sat there, not knowing what to do as she asserted herself onto my boyhood body, grinding her groin against my post-pubescent pelvis.

She pulled her top off, displaying her white, non-descript bra. More J.C. Penney's than Frederick's of Hollywood. "Grab 'em!" she encouraged, as I placed my hands on each of her bra-busting boobs. I cupped them forcefully, gripping her cotton-clad breasts.

"Hey, not so tight! Gently rub them; ease up on the Vulcan grip."

"What?"

"Don't squeeze so hard. Be gentle."

"Okay, okay, sorry," I said, mortified about doing this wrong.

"Let's get in the back seat."

She must have been a gymnast. She dismounted and leapt into the back seat. I opted to exit the car and climb into the back seat in a more conventional fashion. The candy-colored chariot was now a suite. Kristy had rapidly taken off her bra. My taste for women's breasts was acquired as she directed her areola toward my mouth. It wasn't much longer after that we were butt naked, clothes strewn about the Guido-mobile.

"Come on Cupcake, let me show you how to love a woman."

Gripping my hand, she explained, "You have to rub my happy spot."

Cupcake? What is this cupcake business, I thought, *and what the hell is a happy spot?*

As Kristy lay nude across the park bench-sized back seat she guided my right hand. "Yes, just like that, Cupcake."

"Cupcake? Why are you calling me Cupcake?"

"Because you're so cute, I could just eat you up. Keep rubbing and you'll have some frosting, Cupcake."

I didn't know what I was doing except following her directions, but her increased verbal release was provocative. My level of arousal in observing Kristy behave this way was enough for me to stand up and take notice. "Yes! Yes! Yes! Oh yes! Cupcake, you made frosting.

"Now it's your turn. I want you in me. Wait! Get my pants." Grabbing her pants, she directed me: "Fold 'em up and put 'em under me. Your cousin doesn't want anything spilled on these seats."

I'm glad someone was paying attention, because I sure as hell wasn't, I was just along for the ride in a stationary vehicle. She placed her hands on either side of her hips and elevated her buttocks off the padded leather seat. I made quick work of folding the denim and placed it under her raised rear.

"Now we're ready, Cupcake."

There I was, a scrawny 135-pound fifteen-year-old, 700 miles from home, at a horse track, in my cousin Carmine's Caddy El Dorado, gaining my manhood with a college woman I'd met less than two hours ago who is calling me Cupcake! Man, oh man, or should I say boy, oh boy, because that's what I was: a mere youngster. Life, and me, were blowing up bigger than the enormity of the El Dorado. Pointing north, I was ready to cruise the highway of love. Kristy made a good decision to get into education. She was a great teacher. At least she communicated soundly and told me precisely what she wanted. Kristy was a cradle-robber and I was certainly not going to contest her felonious assault.

I did it, simultaneously thinking, is this it? Is this what getting laid is about? Is this the rite of passage, my entry to manhood that all my buddies and I will talk about back in

Ohio? Football practice was less than a month away and I'd certainly have a lot to say during the pigskin drills. Yep, we were so cool, us guys. We would keep a single condom in our wallet, just in case, *mise en place* for sex, if you will. Oddly enough when I'd needed it most, I'd left the Trojan back in the stable in Ohio, stashed away in a sock ball in my sock drawer. Man, if Mom ever found that condom I would have been beaten within an inch of my life. Shoot, if Rosie knew my stallion was running wild she not only would have beaten me, but Kristy as well. Back in those days you were only really concerned about getting a girl *knocked up*. Yes, it's a horrible term, and perhaps dated, but that's how it was back in the day. There was no HIV or AIDS. STDs were known as VD and condoms were worn by those who didn't want their Mini-Mes swimming upstream to make a carbon copy of themselves. Life was a whole lot simpler then. But do as I say, not as I do. No glove, no love: for birth control, as well as health protection.

Our perspiring bodies stuck to each other with sweat as the glue. The Caddy had gone from a chariot, to a leather-rich suite, to a full-blown sauna. Our heavy breathing fogged up the windows like a mirror after a steamy shower. Drenched in wetness, I released myself from Kristy. Our clammy bodies squeaked against the leather as we repositioned ourselves in an upright position.

It was hot. I was thirsty, naked, and in a fog, awkward as a pup awaiting some instruction from my master.

"You okay, Cupcake?"

"Yes, fine, thirsty."

"Let's get dressed, go back to the track, and get something to drink."

"Okay." I really didn't know what to do. Didn't know if there was more, if she was happy, or not happy. Was there something else? I was perplexed by the whole experience and really didn't see the big deal about getting laid. Yes, it felt good. No, I didn't know what the hell I was doing. But I was now a man, or at least I thought that's what it meant to be a man. We got dressed and I turned the key off, ending the music that would forever remind me of my first time. Got out of the car hit the power lock and closed the door. As we got closer to the entrance, we encountered throngs of people exiting the track. The last race had been run and the ponies were now in their stable for the evening.

"Hey, Otto!" Carmine shouted. "You guys have fun?"

"Oh, yeah!" chimed the Cupcake Queen.

Well, there it was: the sign, the confirmation that all went well, because up to that point, I'd had no idea what Kristy had thought of the whole encounter.

"Yeah, we had fun," I added.

Hand in hand, Kristy and I trailed Carmine and Jessica back to the Caddy. As we got to the shimmering land craft, Carmine dug in his pockets for a moment before he remembered and turned towards me. I coolly delivered the keys with an underhand toss and a wink and a nod in a gesture of thanks. He opened the door. "Heeeyyyy, what the hell is this?"

I looked at Kristy. Kristy looked at me. I thought, *Uh-oh, we spilled on the seats.*

"The weatherman didn't say anything about a fog warning tonight," said Carmine.

In nearly a split second we went from uh-oh to laughing hard.

Carmine knew full well his car had become a landmark automobile for his little cousin Otto. On the way home I held hands with Kristy and we continued to make out shamelessly as Earth, Wind & Fire floated above our locked lips. I still love EWF. Every time I hear them it never fails to bring an internal chuckle. Their music generates thoughts about that steamy night in a Cadillac, my passage into manhood in a man-sized car.

Kristy and I exchanged addresses. I was the first and last to write. She never wrote back. That's probably a good thing because Rosie would have beaten both of us if she ever found out—perhaps her sister Giovanna, too, just for good measure for letting her nephew fall into the hands of an older woman. I was more afraid of Rosie than any girl.

Enjoy the cupcakes!

■

I lost my virginity when I was fourteen
and I haven't been able to find it.

DAVID DUCHOVNY

Dearly beloved, I beseech you as strangers and pilgrims,
abstain from fleshly lusts, which war against the soul.

1 PETER 2:11

■

RED VELVET CUPCAKES
WITH VANILLA BEAN FROSTING

2½ cups cake flour

1½ cups sugar

1 teaspoon baking soda

1 pinch salt

2 teaspoons cocoa powder

1½ cups vegetable oil

2 large eggs, room temperature

1 cup buttermilk, room temperature

3 tablespoons red food coloring

1 teaspoon white vinegar

1 teaspoon vanilla extract

Preheat the oven to 350°F. Line muffin pans with cupcake papers.

In a medium bowl, sift together the flour, sugar, baking soda, salt, and cocoa powder. In a large bowl gently beat the eggs, and then add the oil, buttermilk, food coloring, vinegar, and vanilla. This may be done with a whisk, or with handheld blender or mixer. Mix until the liquids are homogenous. Add the sifted dry ingredients to the wet and mix until smooth and thoroughly combined. Do not over mix. I suggest you do this procedure by hand with a rubber spatula with quick strokes until it is just incorporated.

Divide the batter evenly among the cupcake tins, filling each about two-thirds full. Bake in oven for about 20 minutes, turning the pans once halfway through.

Test the cupcakes with a toothpick for doneness. Remove from oven and place on rack to cool completely before frosting.

Makes 24.

VANILLA BEAN FROSTING

1 pound cream cheese, softened at room temperature
2 sticks butter, softened at room temperature
1 vanilla bean
¼ cup heavy cream
3½ cups sifted confectioners' sugar

Split the vanilla bean in two lengthwise and scrape out all the seeds (resinous mass inside the bean) with a paring knife. Place the seeds and the bean in a small sauce pot and gently warm the cream for about 20 minutes to infuse the vanilla. Do not boil. Discard the bean. Put a small amount of sugar into the cream to make a thick paste. In a large mixing bowl, beat the cream cheese and butter together until smooth. Add the sugar slowly on low speed; beat until incorporated. Then add the vanilla sugar paste mixture. Increase the speed to high and mix until very light and fluffy. Frost the cupcakes with a palette knife or pipe it on with a large star tip. For that extra kick of passion, garnish with cinnamon red hots, or for the luxurious Cadillac appearance, use gold or silver nonpareils.

Taste the Freedom.

CHAPTER 14

GUARDIAN RAIL

MUSICAL PAIRING: Goes great with "James Dean"
THE EAGLES, VINTAGE 1974

O N A FRIGID FRIDAY NIGHT LATE one February, the Grim Reaper knocked on my door.

I was with my buddy, John Lansin. We grew up as neighbors and had known each other since kindergarten. John's folks were hard-working salt-of-the-earth Midwestern types. John's father, Darrell, was a farmer, as was his father, not uncommon in my neck of the woods. Your father was either a multi-generational farmer, or he worked for a large industry, like GMC, Lorain Telephone Company, the steel mill, or, like my dad, Ford Motor Company. Mr. Lansin was a friendly gent who smoked a pipe. As a kid I remember him driving down the road in his air-conditioned cab tractor. I'd wave, and he would always respond by grabbing the pipe by

the bowl, removing it from his mouth and giving a little nod—
as if it were impolite to wave with a pipe in one's mouth.

The Firelands Falcons, my high school alma mater,
were ferociously dominant in basketball. Year after year we
ruled the Inland Conference in b-ball. That night was just
another game, playing the Keystone Wildcats, not a rival
but definitely a team who held their own and always brought
their A-game. The game ended with a win for the Falcons.
I headed out with John and, as usual, we were on our way
uptown to Bob's Big Boy—our Friday-night hangout after the
game.

The majority of the landscape in my hometown area is
flatlands. There are sporadic hills, dips and valleys between
hither and yon, but there is one well-known hill—Hall's Hill
or Henrietta Hill. Henrietta, like Brownhelm, was a township
which may have staked their claim to the hill, or perhaps it
was granted such title because of a family named Hall who
lived on top of the hill on the southwestern side. This hill was
steep. Like a giant V blacktop, it dropped severely and rose
just as sharply. As a reckless kid I rode that hill on more than
one occasion on my ten speed. I would pedal my butt off on
the straight-a-way of Vermilion Road before hitting that big
dip, going full bore in tenth gear, reaching maximum speed
before hitting the slight left bank. The bike was my own
personal roller coaster as I pedaled psychotically down that
hill, crouched low for optimum wind resistance. My hands
death-gripped the Maes-bend handlebars, eyes squinted for

fear of foreign objects flying into them, wind at my face, and every care in the world behind me. I'm surprised I never wiped out.

My collision-free record on Hall's Hill was about to expire in hellacious fashion.

John and I knew Halls Hill inherently. We knew it better than the cartographers who put it on the map for the *Rand McNally Road Atlas*. We traveled that road five days a week, twice a day, to and from Firelands High. That hill was no more than three miles away from where we lived.

That particular night was clear. A million stars effervesced, surrounded by an infinite ebony sky. The full moon was God's flashlight piercing the damp darkness. The air was as chillingly sharp as a crease on a Marine's dress blues.

John was a good kid, a good student, a good athlete. He wasn't a rabble-rouser. It was evident he would become a member of the generational farming fraternity. He was a quiet boy, introverted. Had I not grown up with him since age five, I reckon we wouldn't have been as good of friends as we were. Even as teenagers, I remember how conscientious he was. John worked hard with his father, loving the land and reaping what they sowed, season after season. A frugal and focused one, he saved enough money during high school to buy his first car, a 1973 green Nova hatchback. I rode in that car many a time with him, however this ride would be the last in that car.

Although it was the dead of winter, the roads were clear

and dry. Firelands High was a mile behind us. John and I were stoked with the Falcons' victory, headed northbound on Vermilion Road to Big Boy. We hadn't been on the road more than five minutes when we approached Hall's Hill. The eight-track was belting out "On the Border," by The Eagles.

The green Nova was nearing the lowermost part of the treacherous hill. The posted speed limit was 35 MPH. I'm certain John, being the responsible person he was, was driving within the speed limit. In a flash, the car began to veer. We had hit a substantial patch of ice at the bottom of the hill that may have frozen from accumulated snowmelt earlier in the day. John began turning right, into the direction of the swerve. We were headed right toward the guardrail on the passenger side. We were dead-on for a collision course to side-swipe the guardrail. Weirdly enough, I was thinking I would have to exit the driver's door upon impact. The Nova, I thought, would be smack up against the guardrail, prohibiting me from opening my door. I also thought, *I hope this baby doesn't hop the guardrail and barrel roll down the ravine.* The ravine dropped hundreds of feet below us. We were getting nearer the rail. I had a front-row seat to the looming collision with the metal barrier. Strapped in with a seatbelt, I braced my feet on the floorboard, gripped the safety handle on the door with my right hand, and knew in a split second there would be a crash. Halfway through that split second, the Nova's left rear began to fishtail, and John reversed the wheel to compensate. Rotating uncontrollably clockwise, we whirled like an Oklahoma twister.

There is truth to the expression *seeing your life flash before your eyes*. Being sixteen I didn't have much life to flash. I really thought this was it. I envisioned my days at Brownhelm, of wearing the brace, of breaking my leg, of Kristy. Of having sex once and never having sex again, of football . . . My mind was eerily in slow motion as the Nova spun furiously. My thought process shattered like I'd been hit with a lightning bolt. A blast erupted from the rear of the Nova—a sound so distinct it can only be described as ripping metal. The first thing I thought was, *something pierced the gas tank and we need to get out of this car now!*

The spinning had ceased, yet this ripping noise continued getting progressively louder as shards of safety glass showered the back of our heads. With the force of a runaway semi smashing against a freeway trestle, we came to a dead stop. That ripping sound was the shearing of the guardrail. The Nova was gyrating with such velocity it severed the guardrail. Simultaneously, the jagged edge of the frayed guardrail penetrated the Nova from the trunk forward and violently thrust itself toward the front of the car, breeching the back seat. With inexplicable power, the guardrail blasted through the center of the front seat and slammed to a stop, embedding the toothed edge into the dash just above the carpeted transmission hump. That same immeasurable force of Mother Nature that can drive a single strand of straw through a mighty oak during a tornado is the same force that ripped open the Nova from its backside and unleashed its fury onto two unsuspecting boys.

Only one thing trumps Mother Nature: that's God our Father.

I looked at John. He looked at me.

"You all right?" John asked.

"Yeah. You all right?"

"Yeah, shut that off," John muttered, the eight-track still eerily transmitting James Dean from the mangled mass of metal. With my left hand I reached over the metal intrusion and yanked out the bulky cartridge. The irony of that song. James Dean was killed instantly in California in 1955 when traveling at a high rate of speed in his Porsche 550 Spyder. He slammed into a Ford Tudor in a near head-on collision, causing his car to cartwheel and break his neck. The same fate could have easily happened to John or me, or both of us. But the guardian rail along with guardian angels saved us.

We sat there, dangling over a cliff, with a guardrail smack dab between us, half on the road, half off. Had anyone been in the back seat or seated in the front center seat, they would have been impaled, implanted into the dashboard. We were beyond fortunate that night. That guardrail could have easily veered to the right or left during the treacherous turn, picking off either John or me, maiming or killing one of us.

The crash made a startling racket. We saw flashlights coming down the hill, and soon saw an older couple. They walked alongside the guardrail, shining the light in the car.

As they approached, the woman said, "They're Firelands' kids." She'd identified us by John's red and white varsity jacket. It was Mr. and Mrs. Seller. The had children who attended Firelands.

"Is anyone hurt? Can you move? Let's get you out of the car."

John and I carefully opened our doors and removed ourselves from the car. Seeing the guardrail in the dead center of that car, protruding out the trunk like an automotive popsicle stick was a horrifying sight. Mr. Seller stayed with us as Mrs. Seller went to the house to call the police and our parents.

Mr. and Mrs. Lansin were first on the scene. When Mrs. Lansin saw the car, she dropped to her knees and started praying.

I stared death in the eye, and slid through the Grim Reaper's cold clutch. Indeed, it was a miracle that John and I were spared on that nippy night. We have God to thank for that. We walked away from the wreckage without a scratch. As a kid you're invincible—nothing and no one can touch you. You're indomitable and often, like me, defiant. I didn't realize it then, but I know it now: God took control of that steering wheel. He continues to have plans for me.

If God is your co-pilot, move over. Let him drive. The ride is inevitably smoother and far more enjoyable when God is your chauffeur. He is always on time, and never fails to open doors.

■

Dream as if you'll live forever
Live as if you'll die today.

JAMES BYRON DEAN
FEBRUARY 8, 1931 – SEPTEMBER 30, 1955

The eyes of your understanding being enlightened;
that ye may know what is the hope of his calling,
and what the riches of the glory
of his inheritance in the saints.

EPHESIANS 1:18

■

ANGEL FOOD CAKE

It's only appropriate, since Guardian Angels were watching over us that day.

1 cup of cake flour, not all-purpose flour
¼ teaspoon salt
12 large egg whites at room temperature
1 teaspoon cream of tartar
1¼ cups granulated sugar
2 teaspoons pure vanilla extract
Whipped cream, fresh berries, and powdered sugar for garnish

Preheat oven to 350°F. Begin to whip whites in a mixer. Once they become white and begin to increase in volume add the cream of tartar. Whip a little more and add the sugar and vanilla. Continue whipping until the egg white holds a soft peak. Be sure not to over whip the whites. Fold in the flour in thirds with a swift motion. Do not over mix the flour into the egg whites. Once the flour has been incorporated, put into an angel food pan with a removable bottom. The pan must be clean and dry, not greased. Bake for 35 to 40 minutes.

Cake is done when golden brown and springs back when lightly pressed. Invert pan, letting it cool upside down. There should be three tabs on the cake pan which will permit the pan to be elevated. If not, simply turn the pan upside down and let it rest on top of a wine bottle for about one hour. Run a knife around the inside of the pan and around the tube to release cake and unmold. Use knife to release cake from bottom of pan. A serrated knife works best to slice the cake. Serve with berries and whipped cream.

Serves 12.

Taste the Freedom.

CHAPTER 15

LOVE YOU TO DEATH

MUSICAL PAIRING: Goes great with "Born Free"
KID ROCK, VINTAGE 2010

M Y RELATIONSHIP WITH MY MOTHER was tenuous. Harrowing at times, at other moments she was as protective as a mother hen. It was a paradox of good-mom bad-mom, caught in the crossfire of June Cleaver and *Mommy Dearest*. Smothered with love or smacked with a left. On one hand, it was horrifying, on the other, spellbinding. It kept me on my toes and taught me at an early age that you can't trust love. At times she embraced her outlandish son; at other times I was chastised for my individuality. She sung my praises when my junior high art teacher, Miss Coen, recommended her to encourage my artistic ways, yet she frequently beat that creativity out of me because I was a non-conformist. Yes, I was a handful, a rambunctious lad. Boys will be boys, but I was far from a hooligan terrorizing the neighborhood.

Perhaps in my mischievous childhood I was a reflection of her youth. She raised me as she was raised. As a high-spirited teen, I was routinely a recipient of the rod, belt, fist or whatever was handy. My mother raised her kids, echoing her parents' sentiment, *children are to be seen and not heard, not to speak unless spoken to.* Definitely a spare-the-rod spoil-the-child mentality. If you didn't follow the rules, you were unruly in her eyes and dealt with accordingly, which was physically, accompanied by a verbal tirade for good measure. "How do you like that, Junior?" she'd say as she lambasted me. "I DON'T LIKE IT!" I'd screech in defiance and ball up. "Too bad, that's what my mother and father did to me, now you're going to get it!" I'd ask, "If you didn't like it, then why are you doing it to me now?" She'd tell me, "Shut up before I give you another one; do you want more?" It was spitefulness and for years I struggled with the woman whose love brought me into this world and whose loathing wanted to take me out of it. My mother made Cruella de Vil look like Snow White. But this was no cartoon, this was reality. She could be as protective as a momma bear and as ferocious as a grizzly whose roar warned you of an imminent attack.

When I was a teen, she insisted I was doing drugs. She used to call me Hophead. Truth is, I only tried pot once in high school and that was late in my senior year, and I rarely had alcohol, either. Drugs and drinking came well after I flew the coop. She would interrogate me like the Gestapo about marijuana.

"I know you're smoking grass. Where are you getting it from? Who else are you smoking it with?"

"I'm not smoking it."

WHACK! "Stop lying. You're not acting normal, you're on something. What are you taking, pills?"

"Nothing, I'm not taking anything."

"You better tell me where you are getting it from and who you are smoking it with! If I find out, you little @#$%^&*, I will call the police myself and have you arrested."

WHACK!

There were times I just wanted to say I was taking drugs to stop her accusations, but that would have increased the insanity, if that were possible. Believe me, I was more afraid of my mother than I was the police. My mother was the law! She would search my room with an inexplicable suspicion that she'd find something. There was nothing to find. In some bizarre way, it seemed like she was searching my room just to find a reason to beat me. Perhaps coming up empty-handed angered her further. To this day, I never knew why she insisted I was a hophead. Nor could I begin to figure out why she was so obsessed about finding pot and paraphernalia.

Obviously, my mother had issues she never resolved with her parents. She was raised in a different era. You didn't question your parents. It was conventional parenting to strike your children back then. Especially with a family as large as hers. There needed to be order with thirteen rugrats running about. She just accepted it—unacceptable parental behavior was acceptable. Once she became a mother, she never thought to stop the cycle of abuse her parents delivered, and so it goes until someone questions the status quo and stands up for decency and kindness.

Dad was calm and patient, quiet, low-key and rarely troubled. Mom was a talker, a worry-wart and could be consumed by the littlest things. She saw a lot of Dad in me; it would anger her to the point where it would be incorporated in her tirades. "You are just like your @#$%^&* father, nothing bothers you!" I would laugh on the inside, knowing that her blood pressure went up a few notches. Perhaps that sounds cruel, but such was the relationship I had with my mom. The more I got beat, the more I enjoyed pissing her off. I figured I was going to get beat anyway. It was a question of when and what would provoke her. I never intentionally set out to anger her. Sadly, I never had a great relationship with her. It was faltering at best, vacillating between anger and hatred.

As tragic as it sounds, that's reality. I remember a conversation with her, with my dad present. I was in my late twenties and had been out of the house ten years. She said, "You ask your father if I didn't say to him, 'I don't think Otto likes me.'"

"Really, what makes you think that?" I asked.

"That's just how I feel; I can't put my finger on it."

I thought, *you can't put your finger on it? How about the fact that your fists slugged me, your palms slapped me, your tongue lashed me? How about the psychotic roller-coaster you put me on that vaulted me to horrific heights Hitchcock could not have produced!* Incensed, my memory was on total recall, as I thought, *Are you really that insensitive, that ignorant, or both about your motherly ways?*

I responded to her, saying, "You used to beat me as a kid," but she justified herself with, "I beat all the kids."

Mom was a Depression-era baby, where darkness loomed at sunrise and a nickel was as scarce as a white buffalo. I was a baby-boomer, born with the counter-culture spirit of the sixties seeping from my soul. She grew up with hand-me-downs and pasta fagioli every night. My clothes were rock-star bold and I fancied steak and eggs for breakfast. I never comprehended my mother's upbringing until I reached adulthood. Mom refused to understand me and my generation. She would explode about the fact that I had my own car or a stereo, or that I went to a concert with my so-called hophead buddies. "If I had the freedom you had, you little @#$%^&* you wouldn't be here. I WOULDN'T HAVE HAD YOU!" I heard that more often than I care to recall. That was part of her broken record of verbal abuse.

We had a flagstone porch in our backyard. The flagstone continued to a walkway which went to the detached two-car garage about sixty feet from the house. Along the perimeter of the garage grew a proliferation of weeds that were taller than me. She had talked about planting some flowers there.

Our yard was a picture of floral vibrancy. Rosie had quite the green thumb. Her passion for botanicals was extraordinary. A blooming kaleidoscope of petals pleasing all who entered the yard.

I had taken an aerosol can of weed killer from the garage. I was eight years old and planned to do something to please my gardening mom. I sprayed alongside the garage to eradicate the weeds. Spraying the periphery of the garage nearly emptied the can. I returned the can to the garage. A few days later she went to the garage to get the weed killer. It was in the morning and I was eating cereal with my brothers. She came back into the kitchen. Holding the can out in front of her, she said, "Which one of you @#$%^&* used the weed killer?"

"I did, Mom."

Slam! The can was forced onto the dining table. WHACK! Her short arms reached across the long table to deliver a blow that nailed the better part of my ear. "You @#$%^&*. She snagged me by the hair and pulled me outside. I was yanked onto the flagstone.

"Do see you that?" She forced my head a foot away from the stone surface.

"Yes, Mom."

"What do you see?"

"Crabgrass."

WHACK! WHACK! WHACK! She rendered me

immobile by holding a handful of my hair in one hand. She smacked me with the other. "You @#$%^&*. I bought that to kill the weeds in the cracks of the flagstone. Why did you use it?"

Sniffing, I replied, "I used it to spray the weeds around the garage."

"You @#$%^&*. You are not my son. You don't live here anymore. Start walking."

I stood there, face red from the shots from an open palm.

"Get out of here! Start walking!"

I pleaded, "Where am I going, Mom?"

"Go to Green Acres, I don't care, you are not my son, you don't live here anymore. Go! Start walking!"

Apparently, what I did was so horrific I deserved a beating and placement in an orphanage. My good deed of using the weed killer for reasons other than what my mom had intended tripped her trigger. It was a double-barrel shotgun to my body and psyche. The initial blast was the can slamming on the table. The second was the explosion of her open palm against my ear, echoing into the canal and the recoil of my head as she yanked me by my hair. Her volatile discharge still stings through immeasurable layers of scar tissue I carried into adulthood.

Green Acres was an orphanage located in Oberlin. I wasn't the only child threatened with Green Acres. She intimidated all of us, threatening to banish us from the home to orphan status. Mom described it as a place where bad boys and girls go. The way she told it, it was more a juvenile home than orphanage, a place where unwanted children were sent. "You little guttersnipe, they are going to straighten you out at Green Acres," was a common tirade. She threatened to trade us in. As if Green Acres was a clearing house for new and used children. *Parents, if your children aren't behaving properly, bring them into Green Acres and trade up for a love-starved child who will appreciate a loving home. In turn we will whip your ungrateful child into shape by working them in the fields.* So, obeying her, I hit the road. I didn't know where Green Acres was, or how to get there, but I started walking on that summer day. Just the clothes on my back, shoes on my feet busting the tiny tar bubbles bubbling up on Cooper Foster Park Road. I started walking toward where I thought my new home would be. What would happen when I got there? Did they know I was coming? Was Mom going to call Green Acres to say *you can have my son?* Would I be given overalls, a hoe and a spade to work the land?

I walked and walked and walked. I marched past countless rows of corn. It was anything but a field of dreams in my agriculturally rich hometown. It was more like *Nightmare on Elm Street.* I was scared, nervous I would come across a friend, or worse, a friend's parents. I didn't want anyone to know I was going to Green Acres.

I had made it to Bud's. Bud's was a tiny store/gas station on the southwest corner of Baumhart Road and North Ridge Road. With feet drifting, my mind wandered. Just then, a red Mustang convertible pulled into Bud's. It was Paula. Evidently Mom thought I'd had enough mental torture for the day and sent my sister to pick me up.

"Are you okay? Mom's not feeling well. She didn't mean to hit you."

"Okay." I shrugged it off. As time went on, I loved my sister more than my mother. She was Snow White compared to Mom. She was like the second mom in the house. Paula was kind, a buffer to Mom's craziness.

We pulled into the driveway and entered the house. Mom was in the kitchen. She stared at me icily. The relaxed feeling I'd had for five minutes with my sister was replaced with fear. "Go to your room!" she snarled, and to my room I went. I was left alone, but the fear of being hit rattled my bones.

Cedar Point is an amusement park about a thirty-minute drive from Brownhelm. It's a popular park, in fact it's the second-oldest amusement park in America and boasts sixteen roller-coasters. My favorite ride was the double Ferris wheel. I had a favorite time to ride it, too—at sunset, as the bright fireball commenced to sink into the western horizon. My imagination soared, darkness was imminent as Mother Nature closed the curtain on another day. . . that was also the time of day my mother's nature inexplicably darkened. About ten minutes into the ride home, we left our fun-filled day in the rear-view mirror. Looking out of the front window of the car, we were met with a petrifying sight, scarier than all sixteen roller-coasters combined. Mom made a hard right, pulling up to a driveway and stopping suddenly, nearly hitting the well-secured gate. The headlights shined upon a long gravel driveway that faded into blackness. What lurked beyond the shadows of the reinforced metal barrier? She turned to focus her wrath on my siblings and me. "You @#$%^&* if you don't behave, this is where you are going!"

This was Osborn State Farm. Mom had mentioned it in the past. Now we were face-to-face with it after our family fun day. The official name was Osborn State Prison Honor Farm. It was exactly that. A prison farm with nearly 200 acres where inmates tilled the land. "You are going to go here if you don't straighten up you little @#$%^&*." Moments before, I had been riding high on wings of an eagle with the best sunset ever. Faster than you could say *Twisted Sister,* my mother flipped the switch.

There was no physical contact during this ride of terror, but rather an all-out mentally abusive blitz. This was deep, dark, demented behavior. She had accelerated her threat from Green Acres and expanded it to Osborn State Farm, a full-on prison. What was next—Alcatraz, San Quentin, Leavenworth, Sing Sing, Folsom? *I hear the train a coming* . . . Mother's train had jumped the tracks into a deranged derailment of dysfunctionality.

Mom was a smoker. One day she caught me smoking behind the garage. I'd taken a single cigarette from her pack of Benson & Hedges to try. Back in those days it was cool to smoke. I wanted to be cool. Mom smoked, why couldn't I?

Striking the match, I ignited the cigarette and began puffing as I had watched my mom do so many times. I had taken no more than two or three drags when a shrill voice shot through my spine.

"What are you doing? Smoking! Give me that cigarette! You little @#$%^&*. This is my cigarette!"

The fact that I was smoking was bad enough, but when she realized it was her cigarette she went berserk. The red ember at the end of the cancer stick was just the tip of the torch for the gates of hell that were about to open. She slammed the cigarette down to the ground and stomped on it. "Smoking! Lord give me strength."

I knew what was next; I was about to be stomped. Pushing me up against the garage exterior she began to wail, all the while hurling a barrage of verbal blows to accompany the physical ones. "You are smoking and taking cigarettes from me! You little @#$%^&*."

I don't know what angered her more, that I was smoking, or that I'd taken the cigarette from her. She was seething, pulling my hair, slapping me. "Cigarettes can kill you, you stupid @#$%^&* But not if I kill you first! How long have you been smoking? How many cigarettes have you taken from me?"

"This was my first time, I never took any before."

"Stop your lying. You have been taking my cigarettes!"

"No, no I haven't . . ."

"Isn't it strange my cigarettes are missing and you're

smoking them and you're not taking them? You are lying to me you little @#$%^&*. Stop lying. You will obey me, I am your mother! Honor thy mother and father."

It was as if I were getting grilled by a crazed North Korean official to sign a forced confession. "I didn't eat the kimchi." That's how brutally bizarre it was. My dictator mother decided to disown me. "Tonight is the last night you are sleeping here. You don't live here anymore. Tomorrow when you go to school, do not take the bus home, because you don't live here. Stealing my cigarettes, you little @#$%^&*. Go to your room! You'd better have a good night's sleep because this is the last time you will sleep in that bed!"

I went to my room, slipped on the headphones and fell asleep, drowning in my tears.

The next day was Halloween. Mom was revved up at the crack of dawn. I was in the kitchen eating cereal about thirty minutes before the bus arrived. She started in. "Remember, you are not to come home from school."

Empty, dejected, unwanted, uncertain, I wondered, *where will I go?* I didn't know, but I would figure it out. The school bus arrived. I boarded it and sat down in an empty seat. I stared out at what used to be my home, where my sister and brothers lived. I didn't live there anymore. Teary-eyed, I contemplated where I would go after school. I regained myself as best as I could during the twenty-minute ride to school. I didn't want my classmates to know I had been crying. Once the bell rang for lunch and recess, I sought out my friend,

Ken Rause. Ken had been a buddy since kindergarten. He lived right around the corner from Bud's. I told him, "My mom caught me smoking and she kicked me out of the house. I can't go home tonight. Can I stay at your house tonight?" I never told him about the beatings. Ken had an older brother, Jim, four years our senior. Some kids from Brownhelm knew that Ken's mom was a terror too. That's probably why I asked to stay there. He would empathize with my situation. I remembered hearing that his mother hit Jim with a metal pipe that was an extension to the vacuum cleaner. If a few other Brownhelm buddies knew that, chances were all Brownhelm knew it. Somehow my mother's beatings seemed like Disneyland compared to the metal pipe story.

The final bell of the day rang, dismissing the students to board our buses. I got on bus #6 like I always did. When the bus stopped in front of Ken's house I was right behind him and Jim was right behind me. When my feet hit the steps in front of the open folding door of the bus, Mrs. Hamilton, the bus driver, asked, "Otto, does your mother know you are going with Ken and Jim?"

"Yes," I lied. Of course, I lied. What was I supposed to do? Tell her, "No, she doesn't know, but she kicked me out of the house because I was smoking."

Jim told me to go around the back. He and his brother were going to enter through the front door, then open the back door to sneak me in. About a minute passed. "Otto, get in here," Jim commanded. I hustled to the back door and skidded into the basement. "You can stay in my room, it's safe there." Moving upstairs, I quickly followed Jim to his room. He had posters of Led Zeppelin, the Stones, Black Sabbath, and to balance all that testosterone there was a poster of Janis Joplin and Linda Ronstadt.

It was Halloween night. I was supposed to be Spider Man. My costume from K-Mart lay in the bedroom in the home I was no longer living in. There would be no candy for this boy. As my Brownhelm buddies were out tricking and getting treated, I was in Jim's room, eating a bologna sandwich and listening to rock & roll. Ken returned from his door-to-door candy quest. He came into Jim's room. "You want some?" The grape Tootsie Pop was just what the doctor ordered after the bland Wonder Bread bologna sandwich. I savored that pop slowly, slurping the grape-induced saliva, staining my pinkish tongue purple and licking my way to the fudgy center. The best part is when the hard candy dissolved to the point it was as thin as an eggshell, sturdy enough to encase the chocolatey core, yet delicate enough to be crushed by one's molars. It's a superior distinction of textures, crunchy and chewy, soft and hard. That Tootsie Pop provided my first revelation about food contrasts and how textures pertain to the experience food creates in your mouth.

Ken told me, "I went trick-or-treating to your house. Your mom asked if I had seen you. I told her *no*. Other kids were there, too, and she asked all of us if we had seen you. Then she asked, 'Did you see Otto in school today?' We all said *yes*.

I think your mom is worried about you."

I wasn't home, yet the psychological warfare continued. She'd told me not to come home, so I didn't, and now she's asking my friends if they have seen me? Was she worried, feeling guilty, or was she angry because I followed her orders and did not go home? Or did I beat her at her own game and, by not returning home, thus nullify her twisted reasoning that she'd beat me if I came home against her wishes? With her fourth-commandment dogma beaten into me, I honored her order.

Jim broke out a folding cot. "This is your bed tonight. What are you going to do tomorrow?"

Shrugging my shoulders, I said, "I don't know. I'll go to school." We stayed up for a while, talking about things any normal red-blooded American boy would discuss: cars, sports, music, and girls—of course girls. I found some relief that night talking to Ken and Jim. That bedroom was a sanctuary, a rock & roll refuge where posters of rock gods and goddesses served as guardians watching over me.

The next day at school several friends told me my mother was looking for me. A couple of them informed me she'd said, "If you see Otto, tell him to come home."

Boom! There went another mind-numbing cruise missile programed to attack my heart and soul from Rosie's command center. Kids are intuitive and know a whole lot more than adults give them credit for. My friends knew something was up, they just didn't know what. I didn't tell them for fear of retribution from my mother. She gave out just enough information to cause the neighborhood kids to wonder and to keep me guessing as to the genuineness of her comments. Was she really concerned, or was it judge, jury and executioner time? My bet would be the latter.

As school ended, I boarded the #6 bus as usual. I was about to get off the bus again at Ken's house when Mrs. Hamilton stopped me. "Otto, do you have permission or a note from your mother to go to Ken's house?" When I told her "no," nothing else was said. I sat down and waited for the bus to take me home. I remember praying, *Please God, let this bus break down, have a flat tire or something, so I don't have to go home* or at least what I thought was home. *Please don't let her beat me when I walk in the house.*

The bus rolled in front of my driveway. Dejected, I trudged forward, dragging my feet like a swine to slaughter. I knew what was going to happen. There was a large window in the front center of the house. There she was, standing in the living room, waiting for the bus to arrive. She must have been simmering all day and when I entered the kitchen through the side door that's when she hit 212 Fahrenheit.

With one foot in the doorway, she snapped, "Get in here!"

I closed the door and in a flash she was in my face, screeching, "Where have you been?"

"I spent the night in Johnston's barn." Ray Johnston was a neighbor, a farmer who had two large barns on his property. I would never tell her I was at Ken's house, especially after he told me she was asking questions. Who knows what she would do? Take me to Mr. and Mrs. Rause's home and go postal on them for harboring a runaway? The barn alibi, although it couldn't be substantiated, was hard for her to disprove. It would have been easy to slip into either of those barns and go into hiding.

"You little @#$%^&*, you didn't come home last night!"

"You told me not to, Mom."

"I am not your mother! I don't know whose son you are, but you are not mine! My children listen to me." WHACK! "Why didn't you come home last night?"

I pleaded, "I did listen. You told me not to come home last night, Mom."

WHACK! "You little @#$%^&*. I am not your mother! You think you're pretty clever, not coming home?"

I was pinned between her and the door. Cornered, there was nowhere to go.

She began to pull my hair. "You embarrassed me. Last night I had to ask your friends if they'd seen you, if you went to school. Who do you think you are, King Farouk? You think you can come and go as you please? When you go to Green Acres you will see how good you have it here. Except you won't come back, because YOU DON'T LIVE HERE ANYMORE!" Her voice rose to the level of bloody murder. "I called the school to find out where you were. I spoke to the secretary and told her to make sure you got on the right bus! How dare you insult me like that! The gall, the audacity, you little @#$%^&*." WHACK! WHACK! WHACK! She spewed madness as she yanked my hair. "My mother and father are rolling over in their graves because of you. I will beat you to within an inch of your life, you little @#$%^&*." WHACK! WHACK! WHACK! "Never in all my born days have I seen a kid act like you. I will beat you every day until you straighten up, and if you don't straighten up, you're going to Green Acres and I'll get a new son who will appreciate me. Go to your room. You're not getting supper tonight."

If I kept a scorecard on the beatings I stomached, that particular one was especially brutal on all fronts. Physically, mentally, and verbally, she topped the chart. She did demonstrate some level of humanity later, bringing me, of all things, a paper plate with a bologna sandwich on Wonder Bread. She slammed it on the dresser. "I said you weren't getting supper, but it's against the law to starve animals!"

I received countless beatings, searing insults, weathered her monstrous mommy mind games, but there was one single thing I despised more than anything: when she pulled my hair. That was her specialty. She didn't just pull, she would latch onto it, entwining it between her fingers for maximum grip. Once my mane was interlocked in her Darth Vader grasp, she would jerk my head to and fro, left to right, backward and forward, round and round. As if I were a human bobble-head.

I'm surprised I never encountered any neck damage. If it had happened, I am certain she would have denied it. I never let her know how much I hated it, for fear it would become her punishment of choice.

That night, I went to bed and, despite the thin sandwich, woke up hungry. I was pouring myself a bowl of Wheaties when she entered the kitchen.

"What are you doing?"

"I'm making a bowl of cereal."

"Did you ask me?"

"No."

"No, no what?"

"No, Mom."

A long silence stretched between her, the box of Wheaties, and me. She glared down at me, not saying a word. I didn't know if she was silently ramping up to go into attack mode or just fixing me in her crosshairs. Yesterday she was not my mother, twenty-four hours later she is commanding that I call her Mom. Utter insanity.

"May I have a bowl of cereal, Mom?"

Still glaring, she left the kitchen without answering. I finished pouring myself a bowl of cereal, topped with raisins and honey, my usual breakfast. I scarfed the cereal as fast as possible, wondering if she would return and smack me because the cereal question was never answered, and I acted without her authority.

I brushed my teeth and tore out of the house to catch the bus. Apparently, she'd served up enough shock and awe for now . . . until the next opportunity arose. Mother's reign of terror was not exclusive to her children. She took liberties with a few of her daughters-in-law, too. Things got so heated with one of them, my mom was on the receiving end of a glass of water thrown in her face.

It is God's grace that rescues children perfectly from imperfect parenting. It took me years to forgive my mother. Believe me, there were dark days when I hated her so much I wanted to die . . . or wanted her to. There were times when she said to me, "I wish you would die. I will cry at your funeral and that will be the end of it." When I was beaten and belittled, I would retreat to my bedroom, slip on the headphones and turn up the tunes to tune out. I dreamt of getting the hell out that house, of joining the Navy, of becoming a chef. Faith, the power to dream, and creativity was the fuel that ignited my heart with desire. No matter what erupted from my hot-headed mother, the river of life streaming through my being would always extinguish any firestorm she ignited.

It is not what happened to me, it's what happened *for* me. My childhood made me who I am today. What happened to me then is not going to, nor will it ever, dictate who I am today. I choose to be victorious, not victimized, to be a modern storyteller, not a maddening horror story. To live with purpose, not to wallow as a dysfunctional adult. If you have suffered from the hands of abusive parents or are struggling now, you are an appointed child of the universe. Your spirit is stronger than the physical, verbal, or mental abuse any human may have inflicted upon you. What happened to you in the past does not determine who you are today or where you are going. You are a jewel, a gem in this majestic universe, predestined to sparkle. Only you have your brilliance, your shimmering promise. Your DNA is uniquely yours. Accept, forgive, go forward, and shine on, you crazy diamond! I had a challenging relationship with my mother, but she was still my mother. She raised me as best she could, given how she was raised. It's known as learned behavior. She could be sweet as confection or downright hellish, hence this recipe.

■

It's so awful, attacking your child. It's the worst thing I know to shout loudly at this fifty-pound being with his huge trusting brown eyes. It's like bitch-slapping E.T.

ANNE LAMOTT
"TRAVELING MERCIES: SOME THOUGHTS ON FAITH"

Only take heed to thyself, and keep thy soul diligently, lest thou forget the things which thine eyes have seen, and lest they depart from thy heart all the days of thy life: but teach them thy sons, and thy sons' sons.

DEUTERONOMY 4:9

■

DEVIL'S FOOD CAKE

CAKE

1½ cups (3 sticks) unsalted butter, plus more for pans

¾ cup cocoa powder, plus more for pans

½ cup boiling water

2¼ cups sugar

1 tablespoon pure vanilla extract

4 large eggs, beaten

3 cups cake flour, not self-rising or all-purpose flour

1 teaspoon baking soda

Pinch of salt

1 cup milk

CHOCOLATE FROSTING

One 24-ounce bag of chocolate chips

4 cups heavy cream

Preheat oven to 350°F. Completely butter three 8-inch round cake pans. Line the bottom with parchment. Dust the sides of the pans with cocoa powder. Shake out excess. Sift the cocoa powder and whisk in the boiling water, set aside. In a mixer cream sugar on low speed until light and fluffy. Add the vanilla, slowly add the egg a little at a time until well incorporated.

Sift flour, baking soda and salt. Whisk milk into cocoa mixture. On low speed, incorporate the sifted ingredients and the liquid into the bowl, or mix by hand with a rubber spatula. Do not over mix. Divide batter equally among the three pans. Bake for 30 to 40 minutes or until toothpick inserted in center comes out clean. Let cool on wire rack for 20 minutes; remove from pan and cool completely on a rack. Let cool. Spread frosting on the top of the bottom layer. Repeat with the second and third layers and frost the sides.

As the cake cools make the frosting. Combine the two ingredients in a saucepan. Cook over low heat until chocolate is melted and is incorporated into a homogenous mixture, stirring frequently. Once incorporated, chill until cool enough to spread

Taste the Freedom.

CHAPTER 16

HERE'S LOOKING AT YOU, SQUID

MUSICAL PAIRING: Goes great with "Fortunate Son"
CREEDENCE CLEARWATER REVIVAL, VINTAGE 1969

L ATE DURING MY JUNIOR YEAR in high school, my mother dropped a question, followed up with a directive. With her usual confrontational tone, she asked, "What are you doing after you graduate, Junior, because you can't stay here." Junior—I hated junior!

Little did Mom know, I had a plan. I had known I was going to join the Navy since as far back as I could remember. Television shows like *McHale's Navy, C.P.O. Sharkey*, and Saturday afternoon movies, *Hellcats of the Navy, Destination Tokyo, PT 109, The Caine Mutiny, Run Silent, Run Deep,* sparked my interest in the Navy. One of my favorites was

On the Town. I love that flick with Frank Sinatra and Gene Kelly as sailors, singing and dancing their way through the Big Apple on twenty-four-hour liberty. I had it all figured out. Join the Navy, cook on a submarine, use the GI Bill to enroll at the CIA and become a chef.

"I'm going to join the Navy!" The statement broadsided her like a torpedo scoring a direct hit. I shut her up and shut her down. That was the first and only time I ever remember my mother being rendered speechless.

I had convinced my best friend, Jack Vaughn, better known as J.V., to join the Navy with me. I had known J.V. since kindergarten. He was smart, athletic, handsome, and introverted. The opposite of me, but we were tighter than Starsky and Hutch, and as badass too. Or so we thought. But we became bona fide badasses after taking the oath to *support and defend the Constitution of the United States against all enemies, foreign and domestic.* We were on our way to transform from scrawny civilian kids to mighty military men.

On June 22, 1978, just two weeks after graduating, J.V. and I were in a white non-descript four-door government car with our Navy recruiter at the wheel. Before I left the house, my dad said, "You picked a good profession. People gotta eat. You'll always have a job."

We headed southeast to Cleveland Hopkins Airport. It was dark, the sun hadn't awakened. J.V. and I were bright-eyed, ready to lift anchor and set sail for deeper waters. The recruiter handed me a large manila envelope. "These are your orders. Guard them with your life. Here are your tickets to Orlando; someone from the Navy will be there to pick you up. Good luck." With a handshake and a salute, he dropped us off at curbside departure.

After the two-and-a-half-hour flight we landed and headed to baggage claim. I was walking a step or two ahead of J.V. and was feeling so self-important. After all, I knew all there was to know about the Navy, thanks to Hollywood, television, and my brother John, who had already been serving a good ten years by the time I was sworn in. Plus, I had the orders. Dang right, I was important.

Bags in hand, J.V. questioned, "Now what? Where do we go? What are we supposed to do?" About twenty feet away was a khaki-clad cat with a Howie Long flattop. He stood there, silent. Sharp military creases accentuated his honed profile. I knew he was in the Navy. As we got closer, my certainty was confirmed when I saw gleaming insignias on his shirt collar. They were perfectly centered fouled gold anchors with U.S.N. in large block text just below the head of the anchor. He was a CPO, a Chief Petty Officer, aka Chief. Presumably waiting for us.

I walked right up to him. He was six-foot plus, broad as a barrel and thick as a bulkhead. This was one solid squid. Suitcase in one hand, orders in the other, I approached him in all my happy camper naivety. "Here we are, Chief, ready to join the Navy."

The chief locked his head downward and shot me a stare

so startling Dirty Harry would have fired off two thumbs up. He held his intent look. In my animated country-bumpkin voice, I spoke again. "We're ready, Chief, ready for the Navy." He continued to give me his icy stare. This was one bad mofo. I glanced at his name tag. It read *Howe*. Howe was about to tell us how much of bad a mofo he was.

He spoke in a barely audible tone, just the opposite of what I was accustomed to with Mom, and far more effective too. Inches from my face, his scowl slashed right through me. He snapped three distinct orders in a raspy murmur, pausing after each command. I was beginning to think he was Dirty Harry. "Sit down. Shut up. And don't ugly-up the place."

"Aye, aye, sir," I replied, recalling dialogue from old Navy movies. His chilling stare grew colder. Howe moved in closer, lowering himself so he stood brow to brow with me. "Recruit, don't ever call me sir; I work for a living."

I shot back a commanding, "Aye, aye."

The glower grew as I back-stepped away from the immediate trajectory of his glare.

J.V. and I dropped to the hard tile floor, anticipating the chief's instructions. We sat and waited. This was the first lesson I learned in the Navy: hurry up and wait. Wait we did. Slowly, the area became a holding-point for Navy recruits, both male and female, waiting to go to bootcamp. As noon approached, a sea of young men and women, mostly fresh-faced high school graduates, congregated around us. Like the ocean's tide, they kept rolling in. Just like J.V. and me, they were green as seaweed but foaming with hope. Howe stood there, a sentinel standing watch over the flotilla of volunteers who, decades later, still respond to JFK's eternal words, "Ask what you can do for your country."

Chief Howe at last gave a shrill whistle so loud the crowd went silent. "There are buses outside. Everyone form a single-file line." Several hundred people lined up, perhaps upwards of a thousand. There was a long line of busses, navy blue with broad white letters: U.S. Navy Orlando RTC (Recruit Training Command). In short order, J.V. and I were on a bus with the masses, headed to begin the transition from snot-nosed know-it-alls to disciplined, respectful, knowledgeable seaman recruits. We would be transformed in eight weeks.

We received a Navy-issue haircut called a *five-stroker,* descriptive of exactly how many swipes it would take the barber from the very back of your neck to the front of your head to methodically remove all your hair right down to its fuzzy nubs.

After the haircut we were issued our uniforms and the all-important green sea bag to stow our clothes. With fifty-plus pounds strapped to our back, Chief began lining us up to put us in order according to height. "Ah-ten-shun recruits! My name is Chief Howe." I am your company commander and we are going to march to the barracks." Great. Dirty Harry was now my company commander.

So began the first steps of bootcamp. To strip away everything and teach you the only way, the Navy way. Simply put, you shaped up or shipped out. The conversion from kid to squid is difficult by design. Those who swim safely through the demanding mental, physical and psychological riptide are rewarded with graduation and inducted into the mysteries of the deep. They represent an elite fighting force that maintains maritime supremacy throughout planet Earth. They are ambassadors supporting independence and propagating peace for all of humanity. They are guardians of freedom with an unrelenting pursuit against all who threaten it. They are providers of safe passage for people and goods in the ever-intensifying demands of globalization. They are United States Navy sailors.

During the first week, the company was introduced to Lieutenant E. Namel. "Good morning, recruits. I am Lieutenant Namel. My first name is Elizabeth. That's why my name tag says E Namel. Recruits, you are going to learn about proper dental hygiene." With a prop of gigantic teeth and matching-size toothbrush, she began to demonstrate how to brush our teeth.

"Recruits, you have thirty-two teeth that you will use every single day. They will see a lot of wear and tear throughout your life: smoking, coffee drinking, alcohol, gedunk, and eating three meals a day to keep your energy up while you are on the high seas protecting and defending the greatest country in the world. But before any of that happens, during the eighth weekend of bootcamp you will find yourself on liberty. You will notice a pretty young lady sitting all by her lonesome. You are going to walk up to her and introduce yourself. When she begins to speak, she will reveal the blackest, most rotten set of teeth you have ever seen. So, recruits, I have one question. If she is not taking care of her teeth, what else isn't she taking care of?" All of us recruits were flabbergasted by the gorgeous lieutenant's remarks. Her direct delivery packed a punch, adding to her mystique. She had movie-star looks and a klieg-light smile. Yet she was a Naval officer. I fell in love with her, and the Navy.

On graduation day, I was soaring higher than the Blue Angels. The loudspeaker crackled into the scorching celebratory day: "Now hear this, now hear this . . . Sailors, you are now sworn into an extraordinary fighting force with two-hundred-plus years of seafaring heritage, dating back to the Continental Navy. May you enjoy good fortune, fair winds, calm seas and smooth sailing. The Navy Band broke into *Anchors Aweigh*. I was now, officially, a United States Navy sailor.

I traveled to San Diego to attend my MS school. MS stood for Mess Specialist. I would be indoctrinated into the world of AFRCS, the Armed Forces Recipe Card Service, standard recipe cards used throughout all the branches of the Armed Forces. They were color-coded, 5x7, heavy-stock cardboard. The colors represented various categories: breakfast cookery, meats, seafood, soups, desserts etc. Each recipe made 100 portions. I enjoyed my time in San Diego and the thrill of going to TJ, Tijuana, marking the second time I had been in a foreign country.

The first time I was about twelve and we'd gone to Canada on a family vacation to Niagara Falls. Tijuana was no Niagara Falls. Just thirty miles from San Diego, it is also a world away. TJ is the most-crossed border in the world. I have a vivid memory of crossing over a short but high-arched bridge. I reached the apex and there was a little boy. Dressed in tatters, dirty, shoeless, he held a shoddy cigar box. He was selling assorted candy and gum, Chicklets, Juicy Fruit, and Tootsie Pops. He couldn't have been more than six or seven. I'd never seen that sight in Brownhelm, or anywhere prior to TJ. It was my first experience of wretched poverty, right in front of my eyes. Overcome with mixed emotions, I gave him a dollar for a Tootsie Pop.

Beginning my descent to the other side of the bridge, I was greeted by a horde of small children clothed in rags, each holding boxes of candy. They are trained to hit on gringos. The parents and siblings teach these children to panhandle before they can read or write.

Back home in Brownhelm, youngsters were engaged in Little League, fishing, swimming, riding their bicycles to the local Dairy Queen, or maybe were on a family vacation to Disneyworld, the happiest place on Earth. These grubby children in TJ combed the streets on a sweltering day at the saddest place on Earth.

Each child's smiling face of poverty moved my soul.

Forty years later, my heart still weeps, knowing generations have come and gone and remain on that bridge, selling candy to help *la familia* eke out a meal obscured in their cruel reality: survival of the fittest. What I learned in TJ was more valuable than what was taught in MS school. It was my first observation of the squalid conditions that suffocate our global siblings, prompting my head and heart to ask, *why?*

I received orders to be stationed at Pearl Harbor. An intensified sense of patriotism consumed me. Born in 1960, just nineteen years after the December 7 attack, Remember Pearl Harbor was part of my childhood lexicon. Parents, aunts, uncles, grandparents, neighbors, teachers, would recollect the stories of the greatest generation before Tom Brokaw coined the term.

I felt at home there, a part of history in an historic place. Stationed on sacred ground, on hallowed waters, where brave sailors had died, along with the 1,177 soldiers permanently entombed in a watery grave inside a battleship-sized coffin, the U.S.S Arizona. The stories from the old-timers materialized in living color. I was now a seafaring warrior, intimately connected to the past and committed to protecting our future.

I reported aboard the USS *Patrick Henry* SSBN 599. Among the six MS's, one was a peculiar man from the Finger Lakes of NY, Walter A. Zuneck. He was a Petty Officer Second Class and was known as Walt or Wally. He was a wily one and wonderfully weird. Wally graduated from the

Culinary Institute of America, in 1960. He was my sea daddy. A seasoned sailor who shows young sailors the ropes. Wally's nickname was Ma. That was profound irony. He was the perfect continuation of my hospitality training from Cap'n Eddie. Ma propagated the direct link between food and crew morale.

The cooks, the Mess Specialists, were the *Morale Specialists*. Wally said, "You are in a coveted position. Everyone on this sub comes to you to be fed, to be satisfied, to be nurtured. You are responsible for the contentment of the crew. Never forget that. It's not about you, it's about your shipmates and how you brighten their day. Not just with food, but with an encouraging word, a smile, a wink, a thumbs up.

"When we deploy, all these squids have jobs, standing watch and staring at gauges, checking oxygen levels, water levels, sanitary levels, maintaining weapon readiness. Some sit in a shoebox for hours with headphones listening to whales. Others are cramped in the radio shack, bored stiff, waiting for a word to come over the wire that never does. Some are in the control room, with protractors, T-squares and mechanical pencils, plotting our course. All those techs, back in nuke land," he said, as he pointed to the stern, "are monitoring the reactor every second, watching vitals, recording data, ensuring we are safe. All these jobs are by the book, with no deviation, no creativity. We are different than every other sailor on this boat. We feed the men who operate this multi-million-dollar war machine. They will do everything in their power to help a good cook and will not tolerate a bad one. You can pick and choose your friends, because everyone wants to be your friend. Not even the Skipper commands that power. They would give their left nut to do what we do, and don't you think otherwise. When they are hungry, where do they go? They don't go to the torpedo room. *Oh, here you go, suck on this torpedo.* Our job is different every day. Their tasks are dreary, our job is exciting. Many are unhappy, some miserable. We provide happiness. That," he said, grabbing both my shoulders with an emphatic grip and jostle, "is our job. Are you up for the task, sailor?"

"Aye, aye, Petty Officer Zuneck!"

"Call me Wally."

Wally it was, and he remains one of my biggest influences. "Hey, kid," he would say to me, "when you cook, it's like being with your girl. You don't just slip the sausage in the pot and burst the casing. You got to be gentle, you must romance the food. You have to admire it, explore it, touch it, squeeze it. Get lost in the aroma, inhale all the goodness of what you're preparing, heighten your senses. What you are creating is an extension of you. Just like you make love to a woman, you make love to the food. Respect the raw ingredients, devote yourself to the preparation and serve the food with love on a silver platter." He expounded, "Kid, there is a reason why they call me Ma. I put my heart and soul in the food. Sometimes when the shipmates eat, they are reminded of their mother and their childhood. Here we are, on a submarine, hundreds of feet below the ocean. The food you serve creates memories of their mother, their grandmother, their hometown. Nobody else on the submarine has this gift. We're special. Nobody else can do what we do."

Enthralled by Wally's words, I locked onto every one of them as if they were rare ingredients to a master recipe of life, the holy grail of cooking. He was preaching the gospel of food and indeed there is a righteousness in our craft. I figured if this fantastical power can touch 150 men on a submarine, it could touch people all over the world.

I was well liked by the crew because I was a good cook and always put my personal touch on it. Within those two wooden boxes that housed the hundreds of recipe cards, there was a recurring variation on theme, which by some weird luck of the draw, always appeared when I was on duty. It was inevitably some sort of meatball, be it the classic Italian meatball, beef balls stroganoff, Swedish meatballs, or beef balls porcupine, which incorporated cooked rice into the ground beef mixture. Somehow the balls always bounced my way. Given my Italian roots, I knew my meatballs. I started to create my own balls. Pizza balls were zipped up with oregano, garlic powder, bell pepper and then I stuffed each ball with a chunk of pasteurized mozzarella dredged in dry basil and red pepper flake. An Asian variation was teriyaki-glazed balls, with powdered ginger in the mixture.

Word was getting around about Borsich and his balls. It wasn't by design, but by curiosity. As a young-gun submariner,

I created a signature dish that was known and loved by the crew of the *Patrick Henry*: *Borsch Balls*. It didn't matter who was cooking, or the variation thereof, they were *Borsch Balls*. Named so due to the crew consistently mispronouncing my name, Borsch instead of Borsich. They became a favorite at sea. Who knew I would be creating an eponymous dish while submerged in the depths of the Pacific as I plotted my course to become a chef?

Sometimes different divisions would cook. Wally was right: they envied us. While the missile techs had Italian night, and the sonar techs did Mexican night, the real gastronomic extravaganza came from the officers. It was the XO driving the menu. The XO is the Executive Officer, the number two in command. His name was F. F. Jantz, Lieutenant Commander. I christened him with the nickname Skippy. He was a nut for peanut butter, and the name stuck. He put it on everything: on eggs, hotdogs, even steak! The entire crew knew him by that truism. He wanted Beef Wellington and knew Wally could make it.

Unlike the sonar techs and missile techs, who rolled up their sleeves and made it happen with a little MS supervision, Skippy and his crew of khakis were nowhere to be found. Yet Skippy wanted all the credit for the Beef Wellington. Skippy had given Wally a recipe torn from a *Better Homes and Gardens* magazine. "What kind of @#$%^&* housewife recipe is this?" Wally snapped, as he crumpled the recipe and pitched it in the trash.

Wally was showing me tricks I didn't learn in A school. Like a sea sponge, I absorbed every bit of knowledge. The morning we began to make the puff pastry for the Beef Wellington was astounding. I thought to myself, *We're making Beef Wellington, one of the most regal and recognized creations in the gastronomic galaxy!* I don't know who was more excited, me, learning how to make this elaborate meal, or Wally, passing his expertise onto the next generation. I watched as Wally made the pastry without a recipe.

"Open twelve cans of mushrooms, drain them, and chop the daylights out of them."

"Twelve cans of mushrooms, aye. How fine do you want them, Wally?"

"You can't chop them fine enough kid, just keep chopping."

I chopped until a mound of minuscule mushrooms lay on the cutting board.

"Get a pot on the stove, add a shot of butter to it and put the mushrooms in the pot. We're going to make *duxelle*."

"What's that?"

"*Duxelle* is finely chopped mushrooms, shallots, and parsley. We are going to smear it over the beef before we wrap it in the pastry." Wally said another French term, *sec.* "It means 'dry,' the mushrooms must be *sec,* so the mixture will adhere to the beef and not get the pastry soggy." Grabbing the dehydrated parsley flakes, salt, pepper, and dried thyme, Wally substantially seasoned the 'shrooms. "You gotta season the food kid. You gotta make love to it, you gotta enhance its natural flavor. Canned mushrooms are flavorless and waterlogged. No matter what, always make the food taste the best you can."

Opening the vacuum-packed sealed tenderloins of beef, Wally instructed me to save the blood in the bag. "For what?" I questioned.

"You'll see."

We trimmed the fat and cut off the tail ends. He explained that rendering the fat and making a roux with it was because it had more flavor than butter or oil. Wally brushed the beef with oil, then showered it with a 360° coating of salt and pepper.

"You have to season generously, kid." With the griddle on high, we seared the meat. The aroma was sucked into the exhaust fan via the ventilation system, tickling noses and enticing the appetites of sailors, who asked each other with glee, "What's Ma cooking?" We diced the tail ends, placing them in a smoking hot pot to sear, tossing in a disc of dehydrated onion, dried garlic flakes, dehydrated parsley, beef bouillon cubes, tomato paste, bay leaf and a gallon and a half of H20, then let everything simmer.

Wally rubbed the beef with mustard, which acted as an adhesive for the *duxelle* while adding another layer of flavor. Then, after wrapping the loins of beef with the puff pastry and brushing the pastry with egg wash, we placed the wrapped-beef goodness seam-side down on sheet trays to bake in the oven.

Wally added the roux into the simmering stock, thickening it to gravy consistency. He then added the blood, whisking it in in a slow, steady stream. "Why did you pour blood in there, Wally?"

"It's a natural thickener and flavor agent. Cultures from all over the world use blood for cooking. Don't tell our shipmates I put blood in the gravy or there will be hell to pay."

I was perplexed as I watched him pour the blood into the gravy. He offered a taste. It was delicious, given our limited ingredients. I trusted Wally, knowing he had an encyclopedic knowledge of cooking in that crazed brain. He strained the gravy, returned it to the heat, and whisked in a little butter, for sheen and added flavor. Then the kitchen magician showed me a few tricks with the scraps of puff pastry, twisting some to make cheese straws, and with leftover *duxelle* he made a mushroom turnover. "Kid, once you know the basics, it's endless what you can do. That's why you need to go to CIA"

Wally intuitively knew the Wellington was done. "Get me the platters, pour the gravy in the bowls, plate-up the sides." It was *go time*. I witnessed artistry in motion as my sea daddy sliced the masterpiece of crusted beef. The golden-brown puff pastry revealed the deep brown *duxelle* that surrounded the rosy-red medium-rare beef cooked to perfection. I marveled at the components. The crowning achievement was serving the pièce de résistance to the crew: a glorious moment for this young squid. Just a cook on a submarine, patrolling the Pacific making Beef Wellington for the crew under Wally's watchful eye. It fueled my passion. I was nuclear-reactor hot, glowing with pride about being in the service of shipmates and country.

On June 22, 1982, I received my honorable discharge and plotted my course to enroll at the CIA.

■

I can imagine no more rewarding a career. And any man who may be asked in this century what he did to make his life worthwhile, I think can respond with a good deal of pride and satisfaction: I served in the United States Navy.

JOHN F KENNEDY

Greater love hath no man than this,
that a man lay down his life for his friends.

JOHN 15:13

■

BORSCH BALLS

BELOW IS THE RECIPE FOR MEATBALLS, straight from the Armed Forces Recipe Card Service. The recipe has been reduced, but this is the actual recipe I used on the *Patrick Henry*. Feel free to add herbs, garlic, etc. to spice it up.

5 pounds ground beef
1 large onion, small diced, cooked and cooled
1 cup bread crumbs
6 eggs, beaten
1 tablespoon salt
½ tablespoon ground black pepper

Preheat oven to 350°F. Combine all ingredients, mix well. Using a 2-ounce scoop, roll the mixture into balls. Place on baking sheet tray, bake for 12 to 15 minutes. Makes 50 to 60 Borsch Balls.

Hint: before shaping the mixture into balls, make a mini patty and cook it to check for proper seasoning. Adjust seasoning as needed.

Serves 10–12

Taste the Freedom.

CHAPTER 17

R A W

Remembering Anthony Wholeheartedly

MUSICAL PAIRING: Goes great with "Personality Crisis"
NEW YORK DOLLS, VINTAGE 1973

NTHONY, I ADMIT IT: I'M A FAN. So much so, that I am writing this as though you never left us. Even though your earthly vessel has departed the planet, your spirit sails over the celestial body, influencing and inspiring millions across the far reaches of the globe. I have long admired you as the resident Culinary Badass. You're every foodie's fantasy. Chicks wanna do you, guys wanna be you, and every pea-green culinary student worships you in demagogic fashion. I tip my toque to you, Anthony.

Ever since you visited my *Skills One* classroom at the Culinary Institute of America during the Spring of 2001, and subsequently referred to me as a "Culinary Drill Sergeant" during an episode of *A Cook's Tour* on the Food Network, I've held a healthy dose of man-love for you. I'll take that military moniker. It's befitting, the chef of kings and the king of chefs, Auguste Escoffier, after serving in the army as a cook, created the brigade system, the kitchen chain-of-command. Just as Escoffier modernized traditional French cuisine, you revolutionized travel and cooking shows, blending them into a simmering geopolitical, socioeconomic experience for the whole world to luxuriate in. You set the table, but food was merely the conduit as you wowed us. Peeling away layers with the sweetness of a Walla Walla onion, you shed your expertise on ancient history, cuisine, culture, religion, music, social injustice and inequality.

I had been given a heads-up by the PR team a week ahead of time. What a treat to engage the man who radicalized the genre of the chef memoir. How cool for the students to meet the leather-clad, non-conformist chef. The morning of your visit, during the daily lineup, I informed the students we would have a special guest: "Chef Anthony Bourdain, the man who wrote *Kitchen Confidential,* will be paying us a visit."

"Really?"

"Oh, wow!"

"Coooool!"

"Awesome!"

"I love that guy!"

Emotions soared, floating high, mingling amidst the comforting aroma of three eighty-quart kettles of simmering chicken stock. These culinary kids were more jacked-up than a junkie in a meth lab. The news of your impending arrival made for a happy kitchen. "When Chef Bourdain comes in, we will line up, and on my cue, you will enthusiastically say, "Good morning, Chef Bourdain! Understood?"

"Yes, Chef."

"Great, let's give it a practice run, shall we?"

"Good morning, Chef Bourdain!"

"Good, good, but once more with gusto. I want you to remember all the excitement and enthusiasm you had when you first stepped foot on the campus of the Culinary Institute of America. You are enrolled in the greatest cooking school in the world. I want to feel that. I want Chef Bourdain to feel that. This is his alma mater and I want to make him proud. Once more, class."

"Good morning, Chef Bourdain!"

Their words, in perfect unison, intense as a reduction, reverberated from the stainless-steel work tables, ricocheted off the red quarry tiles, and reflected off the mirrored demo table and remained there, magically suspended. *Bourdain is coming to K-8!*

Kitchen Confidential was all the rage on campus, both from the students and the chef instructors. Good, bad, or ugly, everyone had an opinion of Anthony Bourdain.

The students were as green as tots' snot, some as bratty as toddlers too, and were completely oblivious to the imminent horrors and brutality that awaited them in real kitchens outside of the cozy confines of the CIA. They'd be thrust into a whole new world and lexicon. Words such as concasse, brunoise, mirepoix, and deglaze would all become a part of their daily kitchen vernacular. As freshmen culinary students, they couldn't pronounce ballotine or galantine, rondeau or rondelle, sauteuse or sauté. Nor did they know the difference between each of the pairs.

These kids didn't know Jack, nor Alice (Waters), or Charlie (Trotter), or Thomas (Keller), or Daniel (Boulud). But they knew Bourdain, and they couldn't wait to meet the man whose sex, drugs, and rock & roll chef-tell-all spoke directly to them. Like a bedridden patient on death's door, the students clutched *Kitchen Confidential* as if it were the Bible. These chef wannabes needed a fix all right, and Bourdain was the cure. In reading the book, the students were mainlined to a literary IV, nourished by adventures in the culinary underbelly that were dripping word by word into their bloodstreams, creating a self-inflicted culinary stupor of fantasy and stardom.

Anthony, when you came to the Hyde Park Campus to speak at graduation, your arrival was met with mixed emotions among the chef instructors. Some hated you. While hate is a strong word, it isn't the strongest. The strongest is love, but few loved you. There were grumblings, seismographic rumblings, reverberating through the cooking campus nestled in the tranquility of pastoral Hudson Valley, New York. *This Bourdain guy sold us out. How dare he reveal the* dirty little secrets of our pot smoking, cocaine snorting, waitress bangin', Irish drinking, sailor swearin', sub-culture lifestyle? Who is he to cash in on the day-to-day grind and grueling lifestyle of culinary professionals? Perhaps it was ignorance, or jealousy, that fueled an anti-Anthony attitude. Among all professions on the entire planet, there are few, namely, police, first-responders and military, that share the camaraderie of the chef fraternity. We, the overzealous, albeit ego-driven souls with hearts as big as Texas, are a misunderstood and tortured lot. It was bound to happen. After all, so many of us say, "I'm gonna write a book." So why certain CIA chefs had a great disdain for Bourdain is beyond me. Perhaps they were envious and resented the fact that Bourdain didn't do anything different from what ninety-nine percent of all chefs do... except for one thing: he wrote about it. Quite simply, he spoke the chefs' truth and became wildly successful. "Good on ya mate!" as they say Down Under.

So, along comes Too Tall Tony, slaving away anonymously in the Big Apple, as the Executive Chef at Brasserie Les Halles, just another French Bistro in a city of 850,000 restaurants and superstar chefs. Anthony, you put your cash where your cake hole is . . . exposed the dark side of the restaurant business . . . had a runaway bestseller, your own show, and blessings beyond belief. From the ranks of a working-class chef, your rise and fame reached meteoric proportions. Harper Collins took a long shot on a chef who spun a tale of culinary debauchery, decadence and low-down goings on. You anarchist, you sharp-witted, caustic, son-of-a-gun. My man-love for you runs deeper than a five-hundred-quart steam kettle. You are a smoldering stockpot, spewing insidious secrets of chef-dom. The chef world is better because you exposed exactly what chefs do, day in and day out.

June 8th, 2018 began like any other day. I woke up and went about my routine, which started with making breakfast for my ninety-year-old father. While we were each eating our bowls of cereal, about seven-thirty, I saw the headline from CNN pop up on my phone. "Anthony Bourdain is dead. The chef, storyteller and Emmy-winning host of CNN's *Parts Unknown* is dead of suicide at age 61."

Stunned and suspicious, I went to CNN.com. This had to be an internet hoax. It wasn't. The news hit me like a bandsaw ripping through a side of beef. Raw, loud and merciless. Good news travels fast. In the instantaneous world of social media, bad news travels at warp speed. My phone was lighting up faster than you can say "Ma Bell," with multiple texts arriving in nanoseconds. You turned the restaurant world upside down with *Kitchen Confidential,* yet your death was anything but confidential, spreading like a grease fire, simultaneously igniting every commercial kitchen, food truck, and mom-and-pop joint throughout Mother Earth. Your demise sparked an inferno of grief from every single one of the millions of fans who connected with you through food and beyond. We smoldered in sadness.

You didn't merely invent the food-travel program, you owned it. Taking us on a cook's tour to parts unknown, without reservations. You were our Elvis, original and authentic, and an artist. You were one of us, Anthony, and you never forgot that. In you, we lost a brother, a godfather, an uncle, an elder statesman, a heroin addict who lived to tell about it. You were outspoken about drug abuse and empathetic to those who abused drugs.

You had the highest-rated show on CNN, multiple Emmys, a Peabody. You did whatever you wanted, when you wanted, with whoever you wanted. This is beyond rare, it is extraordinarily unimageable. You were rewarded with an astronomical salary and ginormous perks that came along with your fame.

When you left us in France, I watched the next airing of *Parts Unknown* that following Sunday. You covered Berlin, in your insightful, intelligent and, at times, inebriated style. It was ironic to watch that episode.

Two decades ago, when I first stepped foot on the European continent, it was in Berlin. I volunteered to assist the U.S. National Culinary Team at *The Internationale Kochkunst Ausstellung* (IKA), or commonly called the "Culinary Olympics." The episode brought back such amazing memories. I journeyed through Europe with a backpack and a girlfriend for three weeks after the Olympics. With minimal itinerary, we hit Lyon and dined at Paul Bocuse. The namesake restaurant of the chef of the century. He was the supreme ambassador of French cuisine and the father of nouvelle cuisine. I had just met him a month earlier in Florida, because I was a finalist for the Bocuse d'Or American Concours. Although I didn't win, I was one of nine chefs competing for the right to represent America at the Bocuse d'Or. Then on to Paris and dinner at Ducasse, another one of the greatest French chefs with over thirty restaurants around the world. Landing in Normandy to pay respect to brothers-in-arms who freed France from NAZI Germany. Next, we hit Le Mont Saint Michel, the 8th-century granite island commune, stunning in its magnificence and antiquity. Finally, we took a train ride to explore the splendor and sophistication of Geneva.

The last leg of our Euro tour took us to London where we scraped our knees on a pub crawl and dined on steak and kidney pie, curry, and fish and chips. We did enjoy one glorious world-class meal at Mosimann's. Anton Mosimann was a Swiss-born chef who made his mark in England. At the young age of twenty-eight he was appointed *Maitre Chef de Cuisines* at the world-renowned Dorchester Hotel. He eventually opened Mosimann's, a private dining club in the affluent section of Belgravia, London. Housed in a former church, it is an all-encompassing spiritual experience, feasting on what he calls, *cuisine naturelle,* prohibiting use of butter, cream and alcohol. All good things we chefs love to cook with. Yet, Mosimann's focus is on individual ingredients extracting maximum flavor. The creations were indeed heavenly.

You seemed to have it all, Anthony, or did you? No one can ever know what was in your head or your heart that day. What sinister scenario swallowed your special soul to cause you to exit unexpectedly? You were open about previous thoughts of suicide. You had the courageous transparency to lie down with a shrink on the *No Reservations* Buenos Aires episode. Stating, "Suddenly, I'm super depressed for days. It's like that with the good stuff too. I have a couple of happy minutes there where I'm thinking, *life is good.*" You spoke of having a bad burger at Johnny Rockets and that left you depressed for days. It's a burger, I get it—how do you screw up a burger? But it happens. Does that warrant days of darkness after consuming a poor excuse of a hamburger? That gives new definition to mad cow disease. It reminds me of a time when I was cutting my teeth in NYC in the eighties. I was having a slice at a pizza joint, which had the full offering of calzones, stromboli, meatball subs and every form of parmigiana known to man.

A priest entered and sat next to me at the counter. "How's the pizza young man?"

"It's good," I said, in between hot gooey mouthfuls of cheese.

"I don't eat pizza," he said. "I had a slice forty years ago that was so bad I can still taste it." While that priest chose not to consume pizza, I can't imagine life without pizza— it's damn near its own food group. I certainly wouldn't cease eating it because some putrescent pepperoni passed over my palate.

You possessed the swag to sit down with a sitting president! You shared your worldview over a bowl of noodles and a beer with Barak Obama. You made us proud, Anthony! The following week of your departure was the North Korea–United States Singapore Summit. Oh, how I wish you'd been there to represent the U.S. We know how you loved Asia. You would have been the perfect moderator. Dissecting the East-West menu selections at the luncheon, the sweet-and-sour crispy pork and Yangzhou fried rice with homemade XO chili sauce, or the beef short ribs confit, served with potato dauphinoise, steamed broccolini, and red wine sauce. A reporter approached just before the summit and asked, "If you were to cater the lunch, what would you serve?" "Hemlock," you snapped back, which landed you an interview with the Secret Service. Your comment was hilarious to many, but not the men in black. You spoke your mind, unabashedly, damn the consequences.

But food was just the segue, the veritable launching pad that catapulted you into unchartered territory. We went along for the ride as armchair travelers, lusting with you at each unexpected turn, a surprise around every corner.

Who else but you could have sat down with #45 and asked him, "Who toils in the hot sun for barely minimum wage, picking the produce, to keep prices down? Who are the underpaid line cooks that prepare the food into delicious meals for people of affluence to enjoy in restaurants throughout America? Who are the landscapers keeping the greens pristine at your golf courses? Some of them might be married to chambermaids who scrub the toilets, squeegee the shower and complete turn-down service at your namesake hotels. Assuredly, they are immigrants. They are God-fearing, mostly fervent Catholics, poverty-line people who are happy, hard-working, humble humans. They don't have a bad bone in their body. Working laboriously, each meager weekly paycheck is soaked in blood, sweat, and tears. They, like millions of others, are chasing the American dream. With food service being one of the nation's largest employers, and stoves manned by many Mexicans, they represent immeasurable stories of immigrants who crossed the border to make America great. They are not taking away jobs, they do the jobs most Americans do not want to do, period." Maybe #45 would have heard you. Your vocalization on immigration would have made Cesar Chavez proud.

We didn't just lose a chef, a pedigreed raconteur. Gone is a friend we knew and loved through the small screen. We lost a voice for justice, for equality, for proper working conditions. You instinctively knew the power of breaking bread is only second to the stabilizing force it has. That, despite our separateness, our diversity, we are far more alike than we are different. Food is the great equalizer, its thread woven in everyone, connecting us, forming an anthropological tapestry that covers humanity like a giant security blanket, providing comfort and joyous memories.

You were a beacon of hope in a dark world. You loved so many, and millions loved you. Mental illness does not discriminate. Its darkness consumes the famous, the anonymous, rich or poor, doctorate or dropout, man, woman, and child. Suicide leaves the family and friends who are left behind angry, mortified, and in a state of perpetual sadness. There is a hole in their lives, and they will never be whole again. They go on, day to day, existing because they were helpless to assist someone who was without hope

I've been there, had two bouts with depression. The first time I sought professional care and was prescribed Effexor. Effexor works on restoring the balance of serotonin. I had a daily dose of 75mg. While my depression was on the decline, other things were happening to me that I hated. I had trouble sleeping, became nervous and angst ridden. It also brought a bravado of invincibility. When antidepressants are prescribed, it's a crapshoot. The doctor, or you, do not know what is going to happen until the drug is ingested. There is no miracle cure. Most antidepressants take weeks or a month to begin working. The doctor will ween you off the drug as you get better, warning you not to just cease taking it.

After three months, I did exactly that. Quit cold turkey. Honestly, I was fine. Then, eight years later, the darkness came knocking on my door again. Job loss, love loss, death from cancer of my only sister, who was a second mother to me, a feeling of being unfulfilled, and writing this book all took an emotional toll. The pit of death enrobed me. I felt useless, unloved, unwanted. I didn't care. I remember driving through a savage Texas storm with the tornado sirens blaring. Thunderheads swept in like an avalanche, producing golf-ball-sized hail. I was asking God to put that tornado in my path, to pick my car up and hurl me to my death. Despair had settled in so thick I was mired in the muck of not wanting to live, and I wanted out. I seriously thought about pulling the plug. Despite how much I wanted to end it all, there was just too much to live for. I could never murder anyone else, how could I murder myself? There were diabolical days, lived zombie-like in a hellish haze. My bed was my best friend. When I look back at that period, I am angry for that wasted time. Yet that was my mental state, and as antagonized as I was by life's demons, I have forgiven myself.

It wasn't easy crawling out of the pit of purgatory. I owe a great deal to the Friday Faithful, my weekly men's prayer group. We met religiously every Friday at 6:00 AM to praise and worship God. The MOG (Men of God) Squad, as we call ourselves, answered the call to this brother. They were there to support me by any means necessary. For me to refer them as a band of brothers is an understatement. They were life-savers, literally. That is why it is so important to speak to people, friends, family, trusted confidents, medical professionals.

Depression's grip isolates people, shames them into thinking there is something wrong with them, that they are useless, that they will never achieve their dreams. Depression is a sadness. Don't get me wrong, there are mental ailments that can contribute to depression: bipolar, ADHD, OCD, PTSD. I'm not a psychiatrist, but when the shrink told me I was clinically depressed, he didn't take a blood sample, nor swab my mouth for a saliva specimen, or order a urine test. What test does one take to determine that depression is a penetrating sadness due to the loss of a dream job, the ending of a relationship, divorce, or the death of a child, sibling, or spouse? Or even if there really is something mentally off balance in your brain? There is no such test. Yet in this Prozac nation, dominated by Big Pharma, we medicate our problems away. The trip to the medicine chest becomes as commonplace as brushing our teeth.

When depression stormed my spirit the second time, I sought professional care again. After about forty-five minutes, the psychoanalyst said, "You're depressed," wrote a prescription for Zoloft and added, "see the receptionist for an appointment for next week." I left as foggy as I entered—uncertain, angry at the prognosis and diagnosis, and the overall lack of compassion and care from this medical professional who took the Hippocratic Oath. I picked up the prescription and took the 100mg pill, falsely hoping this would be the miracle cure I knew it wouldn't be. That the little beige pill would chase the blues away. That night, after tossing and turning, and with my mind racing, I finally fell asleep, only to be awakened by a demonic nightmare. Persuasive messages encouraging suicide bombarded me like flaming arrows shot from Satan's crossbow.

Those thoughts were so devious, so overwhelming, so formidable, it's plausible to understand why someone would take a drastic measure to end their life just to escape the violently wicked thoughts. I immediately flushed the Zoloft down the toilet and didn't see that doctor anymore. I decided on a more holistic approach: hitting the gym five days a week; a high-fiber, low-fat, lean-protein diet; and getting right with God. It wasn't easy, but the alternative was a living hell.

As Mahatma Gandhi said, "The best way to find yourself is to lose yourself in the service of others." That is exactly what I did. I volunteered for prison ministry. I walked into the Estes Unit, a privately held prison in Venus, Texas. That was a sobering and life-changing experience. I, along with five other Christian warriors, entered Block C. Forty inmates, clad in white pants akin to medical scrubbies, and T-shirts greeted us. The musk of perspired gym clothes hung like a fog. We opened with praise and worship, singing hymns. As it was my first time, I introduced myself and spoke to the men and told my story of coming to Christ. We broke into small groups and discussed various aspects of Christian life. After our two-hour allotted time elapsed, I was overwhelmed with joy, feeling I'd met forty new friends, friends who had been ignored by society. It was the most humbling experience I have encountered in my life. I spoke of my brokenness, and they shared theirs. I have been around the world on mission trips. It never fails, you go to bless the neediest of the needy, and inexplicably, they, the down and out, bless you. That is exactly what happened to me as I left the prison. An overwhelming joy surged from the depths of my soul. Those two hours with the incarcerated men did what Zoloft couldn't do. It humbled me, injected me with purpose, delivered a dose of gratitude, and ultimately gave me a reason to live.

I continued the prison ministry for six months, up until I moved from Texas to South Carolina to care for my ninety-year-old father. The men of Block C created a greeting card as a gift and gave it to me on my last visit. It was a caricature of me as a super hero standing on a beach. The sun was setting on the coastline, illuminated by a lighthouse on the shore. A reminder that no matter how dark it gets, Jesus is the light of the world: those that follow Him shall not walk in darkness but shall have the light of life.

On my chiseled chest there was a letter, like the "S" on Superman. In that yellow and red diamond design was a capital A, for Auto, not an O for Otto. I laughed as my heart wept with exultation over the kindness of these men. All the inmates signed the card, some with extraordinary sentiment. Every one of us is birthed with a purpose, every one of us has a gift or multiple gifts to share. Who would have thought God would utilize inmates to help deliver me from the darkness that was threatening to terminate me and my God-given gifts?

Just as a chef relies on his or her tools, one needs spiritual tools. Belief in a higher power, something that we can stand firmly on, even if we feel our entire world is quicksand. Pray or meditate to a higher power. When you remain still with the Creator it will provide guidance and clarity. Be grateful, thankful, and radiate an attitude of gratitude. Left right, left right, one foot in front of the other—keep moving. God is in the miracle business. He opens doors no man can shut and shuts doors no man can open. These are the spiritual tools that are an absolute must to conquer sadness and its evil cousin, depression.

It is vital to discuss depression. We talk about cancer, diabetes and heart disease. But mental illness like depression is stigmatized. Suicide is on the rise in America. Given the pressures of social media, demands to look a certain way, to have the coolest car, the latest phone, or photos of the last amazing trip halfway around the world can leave others feeling unfulfilled. This comparison robs people of joy, it plants a seed of emptiness, it sprouts despair and grows into a state of destituteness, a spiritual bankruptcy that all the gold in Fort Knox cannot cure. A large part of the treatment, while not easy, is to bring depression out into the open, into the light, for all to see, not let it remain in the darkness where it thrives and takes lives. Friends and family must rally to assist. A text or a "like" on someone's Facebook page isn't enough. Visit, bring a hot meal, ask someone to go for a walk in nature, hit the beach. Being alone is where depression divides and conquers. That is what is so damn perplexing, Anthony. You were surrounded by people who loved and adored you. You were immensely connected, far and wide, with a network of people. You had Sanjay Gupta on speed dial!

Anderson Cooper, your friend and colleague at CNN, summed up precisely and perfectly what the world was thinking. "The man who seemingly was having the ride of his life, in the middle of his life, now suddenly reached the end of his life."

We will never know what global good you could have accomplished. The braise was not yet fork tender, the soufflé hadn't risen, and you had yet to bake our Alaska. You traveled the world, giving us visual and auditory orgasms. During your discoveries you remained authentic, grabbed life by the balls, and drained every drop of love juice from your vas deferens and made a vast difference. Vas deferens is Latin for *carrying away vessel*. That is exactly what you did Anthony. You carried us away.

From one sex-loving, former-drug-using, rock & roll renegade to another, I am reminded of a quote by Jerry Garcia. *"You do not merely want to be considered the best of the best. You want to be considered the only one who does what you do."* That was you, Anthony, an original concept of originality. I miss you.

■

But I do think the idea that basic cooking skills
are a virtue, that the ability to feed yourself and
a few others with proficiency should be taught to
every young man and woman as a fundamental
skill, should become as vital to growing up as
learning to wipe one's own ass, cross the street
by oneself, or be trusted with money.

ANTHONY BOURDAIN

When pride cometh, then cometh shame:
but with the lowly is wisdom.

JEREMIAH 1:5

■

ROSIE'S CANDY CANE COOKIES

I CHOSE THIS RECIPE AND STORY for two reasons. It was my entry for a writing contest Anthony had for his follow-up to *Kitchen Confidential*, *Medium Raw: A Bloody Valentine to the World of Food and the People Who Cook*. This story also ties together our common bond at the CIA, he as an alumnus and I as a chef instructor. The contest was simple enough. Answer this question in 500 words or less. *What does it mean to cook food well?* The winning story was awarded publication in *Medium Raw* and $10,000.

Of course, I wanted to win, or at least finish in the top ten. I wrote Rosie's Candy Cane Cookies and landed in the fourteenth spot, out of 1,949 entries. Pleased with the final ranking, I was fueled to keep writing and hone the craft of storytelling, just as I have cultivated my skill and talent in the kitchen.

■

WHEN I WAS A CHEF INSTRUCTOR at the CIA, one of my students from Mexico, Fernanda Barria, graduated. Her entire family attended the ceremony, so proud of Fernanda's achievements and delighted to be a part of the pomp and circumstance. I had always received great hospitality in Mexico and wanted to extend the wonderful south-of-the-border generosity back to Fernanda and her family. To show my appreciation, I did what I do best: prepared something.

I decided to make one of my favorite cookies from my mother's repertoire: Candy Cane Cookies. Rosie's were simply oatmeal cookie dough fashioned into a cane shape, then frosted with white icing and red stripes dosed with peppermint. I made the cookies, shaping each cane perfectly. To flavor the icing, I went to the campus bake shop and snagged some high-octane peppermint extract, not the drab varieties found at the local supermarket. This extract was as exhilarating and effervescent as an alpine day. To commemorate this event, I glazed the cookies with a simple confectionary sugar icing, using red and green food color for a two-tone stripe because I wanted to capture the colors of the Mexican flag.

The cookies were carefully placed in a shirt box lined with red, white, and green tissue paper. The box's exterior was wrapped in each color to echo the Mexican theme. The Barrias and I had dinner at Caterina de Medici. Our table was festooned by the box in its center. After gorging on our meals in celebration, it was time for dessert. I gave the box to Fernanda's mother, who was shocked by the notion that it was intended for her. Perhaps she thought it was a gift for her daughter, the recent culinary grad. As her mother opened the box, Fernanda apologetically whispered, "Chef, my mother doesn't eat sweets."

"That's okay. I wanted to do something special for your family to return the warmth Mexico has blessed upon me."

Her mother echoed Fernanda's whisper, saying, "I don't

eat sweets, but I will try one." Raising the cane to her ruby lips, she bit off a tad from the tail. She chewed, then went for another bite, and another and another, until the entire cane disappeared. She reached for another cookie.

Fernanda dug her fingers into my bicep, pulled me toward her and whispered insistently into my ear, "Chef! My mother doesn't eat desserts!"

I didn't know if it was health, dietary, or other reasons, but Mama was going for seconds.

"Chef, you don't understand, my mother *never* eats desserts," Fernanda asserted as her mother continued to eat the candy cane cookies. Fernanda's mama gazed at me, intently, solemnly. A single tear crept from her right eye and trickled down her cheek to her chin. "These cookies taste just like my grandmother's."

That remains the single greatest cooking compliment I have ever received. To transport souls to another place, to another time, to jolt a dormant memory, *that,* Chef Bourdain, is what it means to cook food well.

ROSIE'S CANDY CANE COOKIES

1 cup sweet butter

2 teaspoons vanilla extract

½ cup granulated sugar

2 tablespoons water

2½ cups sifted all-purpose flour

1½ teaspoon salt

1½ cups oatmeal

½ cup ground walnuts (optional)

FROSTING

1½ cups powdered sugar

3-4 tablespoons warm water

2 teaspoons peppermint extract

1-2 tablespoons red food coloring

Beat butter and vanilla until creamy. Add sugar gradually and beat until fluffy. Then add water. Sift together flour and salt, add to creamed mixture, mixing thoroughly. Stir in oats (and nuts) until blended. Dough will be quite stiff. Roll the dough into long coils about a ¼-inch in diameter. Cut the coil in lengths of about 6 inches and form into a cane shape. Place on ungreased cookie sheets and bake in slow oven, 325° F for 20 to 25 minutes. Cool. Frost canes with thin white icing and red stripes of frosting. Simply mix the powder sugar with a little water to make a glaze, add the peppermint extract, and brush the glaze on the cookies. For the stripes, after glazing the cookies add red food coloring, placing diagonal stripes onto the cookies to create the candy-cane effect. Makes about 18 cookies.

Taste the Freedom.

CHAPTER 18

LAGNIAPPE

MUSICAL PAIRING: Goes great with "What a Wonderful World"
LOUIS ARMSTRONG, VINTAGE 1967

Dedicated to my Brownhelm buddies and Firelands' friends. My roots delve deep as corn sowed in the heartland, soaring skyward to feed America and the world.

IFE IS MADE UP OF MOMENTS. This book contains two decades of moments that influenced who I am today.

Yet one of my biggest moments came on October 11, 2003. That was the day of my twenty-fifth reunion from Firelands High School class of 1978. Against the concerns of the organizing committee who wanted me to enjoy myself and not work, I catered the reunion. Despite cooking for presidents, kings and queens, rock stars, movie stars, billionaires, superstar athletes, and titans of industry at five-star establishments around the globe, this was my most important and memorable meal of my life. This boy from Brownhelm came home and created a feast for his Firelands' friends.

There was an intimacy, a connectivity, an honor and a privilege associated with cooking for my classmates.

This is where it all started, during high school, as a cook at McGarvey's. I had come full-circle, returning to my roots, sharing the gift of food with my former classmates. With the aid of enthusiastic culinary students from the Lorain County Joint Vocational School, we prepared whole-brined suckling pigs stuffed with garlic rice and lap cheong; roasted tenderloin of beef at a carving station with silver dollar rolls; a fish taco action station; a mac and cheese bar; and a rotating tower with over a dozen tantalizing tidbits all nestled into one-bite morsels on tasting spoons. For dessert, the drama continued with bananas Foster. My brother-in-law, Bob, to this day still calls me the Firelands' Flash. Not because I was fast, because I was flashy. I remember thinking, *Welcome back, my friends, to the show that never ends.* I brought the show and every drop of *Ottoliciousness* along with it. My classmates ate it up, both literally and figuratively. I was in my element and savored every moment.

The organizing committee gave out awards. I received one that was, well, laughable. I was presented with the most glamorous profession award. I graciously accepted it, but there is nothing glamorous about what I do. Sure, I've traveled the world, pressed the flesh with famous people, have had photo-ops with world leaders, but those are small rewards from a hugely demanding, grueling profession that insists on perfection.

You are judged daily by the last meal you create. You work six to seven days a week, back to back, double and triple shifts, holidays, nights, weekends, and the dreaded *cloper*—kitchen-speak for working both the closing and opening shift. You deal with a demanding public with an ever-growing population of gluten-free diners. The world has been eating bread since the Stone Age, now all of a sudden, humanity is allergic to gluten? Guests requests so insane they are farcical. One ordering eggs benedict tells the server, "Don't butter the English muffin, I'm allergic to butter." Really? There is oodles of butter in hollandaise. You're not allergic, you're asinine. You don't need an EpiPen, you need an education. Another time a waiter informs the guest about a sea bass special that is served with asparagus. To which the diner replies, "Can I get a different vegetable? Asparagus makes my urine green." Seriously, no one cares about the color of your bodily fluids. Once, in a fine-dining French restaurant, a guest said, "I'll have the foie gras, but I just want foie, not the gras." Such ridiculous ignorance! That's like going to a Chinese restaurant and ordering chicken with snow peas and telling them to hold the snow.

The life of a chef is anything but normal, and most normal

people are not found in kitchens. It's a lifestyle rampant with drug-induced madness and alcoholic stupors that frequently lead to unprotected sex with co-workers. Throw in hot kitchens, maniacal owners, sharp objects, chefs with Texas-sized egos, outcasts, nerds, ex-cons, wanna-be rock stars, the bearded hipster, the hot pastry chef who is dating the bearded hipster, the guy with so many tattoos he should join the circus. Then there is the addict, who, when he is "on" is the best damn line cook you have ever seen and you wish you had his skills. But, when he's "off", he will sink that line faster than the Titanic. Of course, there is the omnipresent know-it-all, the prima donna who does only what they need to do, who will always butt heads with the bulldog who outworks everyone. Add some low-wage dishwasher/ prep cooks, which are usually immigrants and you have a simmering pot of dysfunctional stew that is going to prepare your meal tonight.

But this ragtag brigade ticks like a Swiss watch. Moving intensely and intently. They are the athletes of the food world, churning out flawless food, with extraordinary execution every single night. It is a gastronomic symphony as the chef conducts the band of brothers and sisters who give relentlessly, all in the name of personal satisfaction and in pursuit of excellence with the goal of making the perfect dish.

Once service is over, stations are cleaned and sanitized, the fish is iced down, the walk-in is locked, and the kitchen is cleansed for another day. The cooks head to the local watering hole, most likely smoking a joint along the way. They indulge in the thrill of kitchen camaraderie with cigarettes and shots after each shift. Then they verbally go through the entire night's service as if they had a built-in replay button in their brain. They explain every ticket, every returned item, subtle nuances during the ebb and flow of service, and the waiter screw-ups—because assuredly it's never the kitchen's fault. From the opening bell to the last order pierced on the spike, they rewind the night and play it back like *Groundhog Day*. They will get home at 2:00 or 3:00 a.m., perhaps make a quesadilla or omelet, and grab a shower to scrub off the kitchen smell. They will look in the mirror and ask, "What am I doing?" The mirror answers, *exactly what you are chosen to do.* Cook, shower, repeat.

But then, moments like this occur, moments like no other.

At the Firelands' High School reunion, this moment crystalized everything I had done up to that day and has enriched every day since. Barbara Karney approached me. I've known Barbara since day one of kindergarten. She is a high school English teacher in Ohio who didn't move far from her Brownhelm upbringing. We were catching up; it had been twenty-five years since we last spoke.

She said, "I talk to my students about you."

Flabbergasted, I replied, "I was the class knucklehead. What could you possibly tell your students about me?"

"I tell them I knew this boy named Otto Borsich and when he was five years old he knew he was going to join the

Navy and become a chef."

Her statement was a lightning bolt crackling with fate and truth. I was stunned. At that point I had been cooking for twenty-eight years.

I never had to figure it out. I never decided what I wanted to be when I grew up. It was decided for me. That is so inexplicably rare. Only the hands of creation can deliver a baby born on death's door and equip him to feed others and deliver the message of hope. *I've been richly rewarded throughout my career, blessed beyond measure, and have seen and done things people only dream about.*

Despite the arduous tasks, the relentless commitment, and sacrifice of being a chef, I wouldn't change a thing. My sacrifices are miniscule compared to the sacrifice my Lord and Savior Jesus Christ endured for the world. It's an honor, a privilege, a sacred trust to take raw ingredients from Mother Earth and prepare them lovingly, present them artistically, and share them unconditionally with those I meet on this journey. Food is the great equalizer, the common denominator. It connects 7,000,000,000 people on Earth through the simple act of breaking bread. I am eternally grateful to be a member of the culinary arts. There is a specialness in this profession that I find downright enchanting. Chefs can create something so exceptional, literally edible works of art, that people will remember for the rest of their lives upon eating it. Food has a way of making us lose all sense of the present to transport us to a place in time, reviving a memory so vivid and fresh it embraces you emotionally, causing you to enter a joyful state of pure, unadulterated bliss. Yes, I will boldly say food is better than sex. Perhaps many who read this will disagree, equating my statement as illogical. But I don't care how good it is between the sheets, it will never transport you, or trigger your memory the way food does. Food can manifest a total mental and spiritual orgasm, not just physical enjoyment. Food is magical, and our taste buds trigger a time tunnel to the past, delivering a memory so vivid and rich it creates a *gastrogasm*—a gastronomic orgasm.

Don't believe me, watch *Ratatouille* and see what happens when critic Anton Ego tastes the eponymous dish. My favorite scene in the movie. That is truth right there. Amen.

■

Whatever you are, be a good one.

ABRAHAM LINCOLN

Now the God of hope fill you with all joy and peace in believing, that ye may abound in hope, through the power of the Holy Ghost.

ROMANS 15:13

■

CHAPTER 19

FORTY WORDS FROM FORTY FRIENDS

MUSICAL PAIRING: Goes great with "You've Got a Friend in Me"
RANDY NEWMAN, VINTAGE 1995

On the following pages are sentiments written by friends from my garden of life. Some go as far back as kindergarten. Others took root later in life. Throughout the ages, we have blossomed together on this journey. Thank you for beautifying the world. May your soul perpetually bloom and sashay like a breeze-kissed daffodil on an April day.

1 Ripe tomatoes and parmesan cheese are used to enhance the umami flavor profile of a pasta dish. Likewise, Chef Otto's knowledge and experience inspire one to search deeply within oneself to extract and develop the individual gift within oneself.

BASHAR AMMARI, COPPELL, TEXAS

2 Otto is without filter. Loud and proud, a fault for many but greatly unique in him. A man of many friends and no enemies. Sincere, he molds himself to those around him. Walking in your shoes and carrying your load.

JAIME BLANCO, TEMECULA, CALIFORNIA

3 Otto's world is one giant costume party. Light enters his soul emitting a rainbow to all he encounters. His cosmic kaleidoscope radiates a fun personality, a spirit of love, kindness, and an endless loyalty to country and friend.

KELLY BRADLEY, WESTLAKE, TEXAS

4 Otto, the most memorable character I ever met. That opinion was formed at first meeting! Then confirmed during the one-and-a-half years he lived in our home. Perpetually upbeat, Otto brings supreme flair to his relationships and cooking.

SCOTT BRADLEY, WESTLAKE, TEXAS

5 I met an outspoken, confident, vibrant, extremely talented, Otto in 1990. Our common bond was cuisine. His heart is feeding impoverished souls worldwide. Otto has a genuine relationship with God. He is a different chef, man, and whole being.

FRED BRASH, NORWALK, CONNECTICUT

6 Truthful. Honest. Faithful. Giving. Musical. Sharing. Spiritual. Carefree. Listener. Adventurer. Intelligent. Seeker. Friend. Energetic. Loyal. Beautiful. Intense. Loving. Caring. Funny. Patriotic. Incredible. Zealous. Enthusiastic. Talker. Agile. Believer. Amazing. Determined. Entertainer. Hysterical. Eccentric. Bright. Special. Foresight. Resilient. Devoted. Outlandish. Teacher. Veteran.

DAWN COLLIER, CHARLOTTE, NORTH CAROLINA

7 He cooked hundreds of pounds of gumbo feeding 400 children, the poorest among the poor. They were delighted, enjoying the food and his presence. Thank you, Chef Otto, for your heart and cooking for us. You are a humble man.

PASTOR BOB CUENCA, LAPU-LAPU CITY, PHILIPPINES

8 Otto will forever be that boy from Brownhelm who would be a chef. It's wonderful to watch his childhood dreams come true. A unique small-town boy who sprouted into an oak and never forgot where he came from.

BONNIE CUTCHER, WELLINGTON, OHIO

9   Chef Otto propels us on his personal journey of infinite culinary and spiritual exploration. His version of being alive is larger than life. With an appetite for adventure, cuisines, and cultures, his shared experiences nourish the mind, body, and soul.

MAUREEN DALY, NEW YORK, NEW YORK

10   While shopping for a whisk, he asked me what I was going to do with it. Through thirty years of abiding friendship, I hope, Otto, my mentor, that I took your guidance and made you proud. You changed my life.

MICHELLE MATTHEWS, SANDUSKY, OHIO

11   Chef Otto is committed to feeding people, nourishing mind, body, and soul. Dedicated to ensuring our brothers and sisters have enough to eat. Enjoy learning from his cooking, his story, his example, then join his quest to achieve zero hunger.

MAX FINBERG
DIRECTOR AT THE UN'S WORLD FOOD PROGRAM,
AND FORMERLY WITH THE WHITE HOUSE, AMERICORPS VISTA,
USDA, AND THE ALLIANCE TO END HUNGER

12   Chef Otto, a solider, respectful, diligent, a working man. God-fearing, dreamer, blue-collar minded, resourceful, kid-loving, completely whacked adventurer, driven culinarian, fervent patriot. Or, simply put, a man on the road filling life's daily personal *mise en place* list.

GEORGE FISTROVICH, NAPLES, FLORIDA

13   A long time ago my friend Otto helped me understand that, as a cook, my most important tool in the kitchen is my palate. Proper seasoning is paramount. If you're not tasting your food, you're not doing your job.

GREG FLANAGAN, VERO BEACH, FLORIDA

14   A unique human being, a philanthropist with a desire to travel and help the needy, an out-of-the-box extrovert are some of the descriptions given to Chef Otto. Indeed, a fascinating man with a compelling story to tell.

DR. BILLY GALLAGHER, JOHANNESBURG, SOUTH AFRICA

15   An unforgettable experience to work under Chef Otto during the grand opening of Mardan Palace in Turkey. Friendly, inspiring, and strange, his leadership orchestrated an efficient, cooperative, and highly trained culinary team. I look forward to working with him again.

AMJAD GHANDOOR, AMMAN, JORDAN

16   I have felt and experienced Otto's sincere and loving spirit for life. The stories and experiences he speaks about in this amazing book will have you also feeling his anguish, struggles, and trials he's had along his journey of life.

BETTYANN GOLDEN, LAS VEGAS, NEVADA

17 What amazes me about Otto is his positivity. When life gives him lemons, he makes lemonade, lemon bars, lemon meringue pie et cetera, get the picture. He finds a way to go beyond surviving while helping others thrive along the way.

BOB GOLDEN, LAS VEGAS, NEVADA

18 Knowing Otto is loving Otto. From his fun crazy attitude, his love of life, and his genius in creating culinary delights. To his clothes and the amazing ways he chooses to wear them. What about his hair? It's pure Otto!

PAUL & ANNEMARIE HANNAN, SYDNEY, AUSTRALIA

19 Otto lives life to the extreme. In elementary school I watched him conquer a disability. We stood tall as teammates for Firelands Falcons football and joined the Navy together. His life is a bestseller, and this book, like Cleveland, ROCKS!

ROD JEWELL, WICKLIFFE, OHIO

20 Passionate about the culinary world. He is never too busy to lend a hand, meets challenges with optimism and a can-do attitude. A veteran and humanitarian, his love of God, country, and the world is an inspiration to all he meets.

FARMER LEE JONES, MILAN, OHIO

21 Talks faster than any native New Yorker! My first culinary mentor, exuberant, a patriot. A champion for hunger issues and compassionate for those less fortunate. Curious, dependable, humorous, a volunteer, an insatiable adventurer of the highest order.

DANIELLE KAYE, NEW YORK, NEW YORK

22 Ottomaniac: The embodiment of adventure, I could listen to his stories for hours and would pay to hear his laugh! Anyone who is fortunate to cross paths with this uniquely gifted, passionate, sacrificial, amazing man should consider themselves truly blessed!

RENATA T. KNIGHT, KELLER, TEXAS

23 "Chefs are cut from a different cloth." Chef Otto inspired me 20 years ago. I became a tough Head Chef in a man's world. He was a big part of my journey and I remain eternally thankful for him.

TIFFANY FORBES LINDEN, NASSAU, BAHAMAS

24 Otto is zealous about food and life! Loyal and generous to friends and family. Capable of such love he would joyfully feed the world if he could. I wish everyone had his heart. The world would be a better place.

ANDRIA LITTO, LOS ANGELES, CALIFORNIA

25 Chef Otto is perfectly complex, like an over-stuffed NY deli sandwich! His very first steps were giant ones, he was born to beat the odds and whip the egg whites! A patriot, lover of all people, and culinary badass!

REBA MCCONNELL, VIRGINIA BEACH, VIRGINIA

26 Otto is an endless source of enthusiasm, a wondrous spirit. From cooking on a nuclear submarine, to *Top Chef,* to being employed at the CIA as a Professor of Culinary Arts without any formal education—Otto always captivates!

MARTI MONGEILLO, GROVNER, NORTH CAROLINA

27 Chef Otto, he cooks the best American food and encouraged me to embrace all types of cuisine. An inspiration to turn my weakness into strength. His support made me a stronger person and I will forever be grateful.

TAE SIVA NAPHAVARANONTH, BANGKOK, THAILAND

28 I have always been in love with food. In my quest to find the best culinary school in the world, I enrolled at the CIA. I also found a good friend and a great teacher. Thank you, Chef Borsich.

SERGIO PEREZ, QUITO, ECUADOR

29 Everyone needs a friend like Otto. He is the most unforgettable character in my life. A fascinating soul filled with warmth and friendship. His love of country is without boundaries. Otto has taught me to dance in the rain.

ROXANNE PIZZETTI, DALLAS, TEXAS

30 Otto G. Borsich II, a great chef, a skillful instructor and guru, a passionate motivator, a discipline junkie full of energy with lots of humor and compassion. A hearty patriot whom I am honored to call my friend.

DEGAN SEPTOADJI , SUPRIJADI, BALI, INDONESIA

31 Otto seems to have been created to share encouragement, inspiration, love, and light to others. Humble, selfless, gracious, he moves through the world genuinely loving, caring for, and uplifting those he meets as enthusiastically as anyone I have ever met.

DUG SHELBY, PASO ROBLES, CALIFORNIA

32 A rich friendship dating back to 1983, when Otto was an apprentice at the Pierre Hotel. We've shared thousands of work hours, national and international competitions. He tirelessly puts others first. An excellent cook, my mentee, an inspiration to culinarians.

MICHAEL SKIBITCKY, RED HOOK, NEW YORK

33 A Chef who can write? Not only yes, but hell yes! His writing style is so unique and entertaining. Made me laugh. Made me cry. Made me think. Can't ask for more than that from a good read.

CHRISTINE CROCKETT SMITH, DALLAS, TEXAS

34 An old soul, a heart of gold, talented beyond belief, humanitarian, worldwide traveler. Someone I'm proud to say is a dear much-loved old friend of 40-plus years. I knew you would make your dreams come true.

CHERYL SHAFFER SZCZEPANSKI, AMHERST, OHIO

35 Otto, the man—behind all the dreams, behind all the faith, behind his boisterous laugh. Always a gentleman. The talent—behind the chef jacket, behind the camera, behind the words. A truly unique being!

DEBORAH LLEWYN COLE, ROANOKE, TEXAS

36 Solemn sailors were saying aloha to loved ones. Otto burst onto the submarine with an entourage. Submerged for months underwater, forty years later he remains an enthusiastic kid from Ohio. Loyal friend, proud American, not a bad chef either.

GERRY TUOHY, WILLIAMSBURG, VIRGINIA

37 Because of Otto Borsich I encountered the Divine during a darkness within my life. He is laughter and joy, courageous and outrageous, brilliant and funny. He loves God, humanity and Bruce Springsteen. Otto's friendship is sweet music to my life.

EILEEN WALKER, GRAPEVINE, TEXAS

38 A distinctive individual. His style, intellect, sense of humor, and chef skills differentiate him. An amazing storyteller, I've heard him speak about world hunger. Inspirational, he implores chefs into action to feed those in need, to bless and be blessed.

TIM WASYLKO , OTTAWA, ONTARIO, CANADA

39 Otto encompasses all five senses. His talent for making the aroma and taste of food come alive, his laugh rings across kitchens and continents, beholding his colorful personality while entertaining people. May this autobiography awaken the sixth sense, your heart.

HELENE & GREG WALTON
INTERNATIONAL DEVELOPMENT WORKERS, CANILLÁ,
DEPARTMENT OF EL QUICHÉ, GUATEMALA, CENTRAL AMERICA

40 God placed one word on my heart for Otto. *Tushiyyah* (too-shee-yaw'); Hebrew in origin, it's a dual definition. The effect of sound wisdom and abiding success. *Counsel is mine, and sound wisdom; I am understanding; I have strength.* PROVERBS 8:14

DANE YOUNG, FT WORTH, TEXAS

RECIPE FOR A HAPPY LIFE

AN ABUNDANCE OF LOVE. You can never have too much love.

A TON OF PATIENCE. Things don't always work out as you thought. Sometimes they work out better.

A BOATLOAD OF PERSISTENCE. Nothing comes easy in life, but as the stream wears down the rock it becomes polished.

A BUSLOAD OF FAITH. You gotta believe, and believe in something bigger than yourself.

AN OVERFLOWING PERSONAL STYLE. God made you to stand out, why blend in?

UNLIMITED FORGIVENESS. We all want to be forgiven, yet at times we are resistant to be the one who forgives.

A HEALTHY BALANCE. We all have a friend named Jack, he can be so dull because he works all the time. Don't be a Jack.

DOLLARS AND CENTS make good sense. Save for a rainy day, you never know when a personal tsunami will hit.

INTEGRITY. The best way to keep your word is to not give it. When you do, honor it.

VOLUNTEER. Somebody somewhere needs you.

MORE BOOKS, LESS TV. My father called it an idiot box for a reason.

YOUR ATTITUDE determines your altitude, and on the topic of attitude, have an attitude of gratitude. Be thankful for what you have.

NEVER GIVE UP. Your best days are ahead of you.

FOCUS. Remove yourself from the periphery; tune in with the intensity of a laser beam.

BE HAPPY. It's a choice every day.

LAUGHTER. It truly is the best medicine, the least expensive, too. It's right up there with love—you can never have enough.

Taste the Freedom.

OTTO BORSICH

R AISED IN THE HEARTLAND, Otto Borsich was destined to be a chef. With a mile-wide smile and a heart as big as Texas, he radiates his livelihood with incomparable gusto and is a humble servant who shares his gift of food with all who cross his path on life's journey. A patriot of the highest order, he served and cooked aboard a nuclear submarine in the US Navy. As a self-professed International Culinary Ambassador, he has traveled the world sharing the gospel of American Regional Cuisine to the penniless, not only delivering delicious food for their enjoyment and sustenance, but nourishing minds and souls with his infectious laugh and inspirational anecdotes.

He is a firm believer and living example of utilizing the gift(s) we are born with to improve the lives of others and leave the world a better place than what we inherited. From the gift of food to the art of storytelling, his Otto-Biography, *A Chef is Born,* is the captivating story of a small-town boy who overcame phenomenal obstacles and followed his true north star to become a chef.

RECIPE INDEX

CPSIA information can be obtained
at www.ICGtesting.com
Printed in the USA
JSHW050513230622
27398JS00001B/3